THE EAGLE
COOKBOOK

RECIPES FROM THE
ORIGINAL GASTROPUB

THE EAGLE
COOKBOOK

RECIPES FROM THE
ORIGINAL GASTROPUB

DAVID EYRE
& THE EAGLE CHEFS

A.

ABSOLUTE PRESS

First published as *Big Flavours, Rough Edges* by Hodder Headline in 2001.

This revised edition with additional recipes first published in 2009 by

Absolute Press
Scarborough House
29 James Street West
Bath BA1 2BT
Phone 44 (0) 1225 316013
Fax 44 (0) 1225 445836
E-mail info@absolutepress.co.uk
Website www.absolutepress.co.uk

Publisher Jon Croft
Commissioning Editor Meg Avent
Art Director and Designer Matt Inwood
Design Assistant Claire Siggery
Publishing Assistant Andrea O'Connor
Editor Jane Middleton
Photographer Lara Holmes
Food Stylist Trish Hilferty

ISBN: 9781906650056

Printed and bound in England
by Butler Tanner and Dennis

A note about the text
This book was set using Helvetica Neue and Century. Helvetica was designed in 1957 by Max Miedinger of the Swiss-based Haas foundry. In the early 1980s, Linotype redrew the entire Helvetica family. The result was Helvetica Neue. The first Century typeface was cut in 1894. In 1975 an updated family of Century typefaces was designed by Tony Stan for ITC.

CONTENTS

FOREWORD BY FAY MASCHLER

There are people of legal drinking age out there whose entire life has held out the possibility of going to a gastropub. They could not begin to imagine the amazement, the delight – the appetite – that greeted the arrival of the Eagle in its new incarnation in early 1991.

In an *Evening Standard* article of 19 February of that year, in a section that included news of a rapprochement between Margaret, Duchess of Argyll and her only daughter Frances, Duchess of Rutland and speculation as to how Prince Charles and Princess Diana would celebrate their 10th wedding anniversary – as well as an assessment of how designer shops were weathering the recession – I reviewed the Eagle. I reported that two young chaps, Michael Belben and David Eyre (chef), who in the 1980s had been working at Smith's and Melange restaurants in Covent Garden, had benefited from a cheap near end-of-lease deal in a Farringdon pub where décor was 'practically non-existent' but the food 'notable and achievable within the confined kitchen and service space'.

What I didn't know then is that Mike and David had put in £5,000 each and the brewery had lent them £10,000. These are start-up costs to nowadays make one gasp and stretch one's eyes. Fed up with working in restaurants in which they couldn't afford to eat, the pair had put the two and two together that no one previously had figured would make four: pubs had full-on licenses meaning you could drink without eating. Restaurants had to abide by the law of the time (enthusiastically supported by the brewing lobby), which meant that alcohol could not be served except with food. Introducing admirable food into a pub was the simple, elegant, empathetic and relatively cheap solution.

'Never forget it's a pub' was, and is, their manifesto. Certain aspects of pubs such as gaming machines, optics, sticky carpets, sausages and pies in a hot box and Scotch eggs with greying yolks rattling around inside an orange crumbed carapace could and would be dumped. But there was no need to import restaurant constraints such as bookings, linen, credit cards, service charge, table numbers and a bill. You still pay up front with cash for food and drink at the Eagle and, according to its owners, this makes customers more forgiving of any longeurs in the delivery. Well, maybe.

Pictograms and nicknames were used for the dissemination of orders taken at the bar. HMHS was Half-Man Half-Schoolboy, HM was Hairy Microbe. DGD was Day-Glo Derek. To tally up the number of customers fed the pile of car boot sale mis-matched plates was counted. There was no compulsion for customers to eat. As you might infer, the *Guardian* and *Observer* offices proved a fertile ground for growing supporters, as did the nearby headquarters of *Arena* and *The Face*.

Now that gastropubs are legion none of this sounds extraordinary but the Eagle and the attitudes of its owners turned over a trailblazing new leaf in eating out. David Eyre has summed up the style of the food as 'On holiday all around the Mediterranean'. You might think, just a minute, a pub is such a British institution. But what do the British do? They go on holiday all around the Mediterranean. Eighteen years ago, buffalo mozzarella arrived courtesy of DHL and pesto was a revelation. Eyre claims to have been the first to make it fresh in a restaurant, well in a pub anyway. Now the recipes in this book encapsulate exactly how we like to eat, both out and at home; no fuss, no muss.

Before writing this, I met Eyre and Belben for lunch at the River Café. It was a fitting place. Pedro Chaves, their first hired chef at the Eagle came from that similarly seminal restaurant where the driving spirit is that of a family. Cooking together is one recipe for a happy family who also learn from each other. You start by podding and shucking the broad beans. You go on to understand how to make a risotto flavoured with the emerald embryos plus mint. You feel satisfied. Maybe you then think about wanting to open your own pub or restaurant but you stay in touch or, indeed, in business. The principles of the Eagle live on in associated businesses like the Anchor & Hope and Great Queen Street.

Over its long life – restaurant years are like dog years, you multiply by seven – there have been only three head chefs at the Eagle, David Eyre, Tom Norrington-Davies (now head chef at Great Queen Street) and the current incumbent Ed Mottershaw. The energy which, mercifully launched a thousand imitators, stays constant. David Eyre can have the last word on the Eagle – at least until the next edition of Eagle recipes is published – 'The food should not in any way be exquisite. It is not a dining experience'. Thank God for that, I say.

Fay Maschler
Restaurant critic of the *London Evening Standard*
June 2009

'BIG FLAVOURS & ROUGH EDGES'

I've always been more than a little bemused about why the Eagle was regarded as such a radical notion when it opened, and then how it became so influential in changing what we all now expect from a pub. To my partner, Mike Belben, and me, it was always obvious that simple, intelligent food was what London pubs lacked. 1990 was not a happy time for many London restaurants; the recession was hurting badly and, notwithstanding our desperation to have our own restaurant, we just couldn't see how a medium-sized, medium-priced operation could make any money. Rents and premiums were ridiculous, the costs of providing all the expected trappings of service couldn't be justified, and it was illegal to sell alcohol to anyone not eating a full meal. Besides, we didn't have the minimum of £250,000 needed to open a simple restaurant. Fortunately, in the wake of the Monopolies and Mergers Commission's ruling on the major breweries' tenanting practices, there were for the first time a number of pubs available with new-style leases.

The Eagle was the first and cheapest dead pub we found. The lack of trade was such that we had to stand on tables outside peering over dark curtains at the gloom within. But beneath the sad grime we could see an attractive, if small, room with huge windows and a maple floor. It also had the fine brick façade of an early Truman corner-sited pub. Three weeks later we had our cheeky offer accepted by the outgoing leasees, had taken out a small bank loan and borrowed a further £5,000 from each of our families. My brother became the only employee, and after three weeks of scrubbing and throwing out standard brewery pub kit we had our opening night.

There was a major constraint on our aim of providing my idea of pub food. The existing kitchen behind the bar measured 8 feet by 5 feet. There was a kitchen in the flat – well, it had an oven – but on the ground floor all we had was a small domestic fridge, a small microwave, a small eye-level grill of sorts, a domestic sink and a two-burner hob. It was early January and it would be Easter before we could afford to stretch the bar to make the kind of kitchen we needed. No matter, the menu would have a soup; sausages bought twice daily from the established Italian grocer's, Gazzano & Son, next door; crostini from the grill, loaded with vegetables patiently cooked under the same grill all morning; a steak sandwich from my Mozambique childhood cooked on one of the burners (the other was needed for our Vesuvian coffee pots); a salad of some kind; and from the flat at 12.30 would come a casserole and an oven dish.

Into this came our first chef, Pedro, via the River Café, and together we would somehow cook up to 80 lunches before having to shop for the evening. But the Eagle's food really took off after that Easter, with a kitchen that now had a chargrill, a cooker and a proper fridge. Shortly after, we gained a prep room downstairs, but the kitchen still had space for only two cooks. The menu's key feature has thus required to cook 120 lunches in 120 minutes, then this would preclude starters and desserts; besides it was to remain a pub, and not become a restaurant.

As the reviews started coming in (we made excellent copy), we were approached by some brilliant suppliers. We were now able to access fantastic Spanish, Italian and Portuguese products, and fish came in from several small outfits, but I am most thankful for the arrival of Greg Wallace and Terry Bailey of George Allan's Greengrocers. Remember that as recently as 1991, chefs just couldn't get the stuff they use today. These guys eschewed the carrots and baking potatoes mentality of New Covent Garden. Herbs arrived in vast bunches, tomatoes and peppers were ripened on a vine in some sunny land and not in a Dutch hothouse, tiny purple artichokes and fat wet garlic were seen for the first time. And then the quality of the chefs that came to me for a job: some had had years of professional experience but were anxious to leave the hierarchies and tedium of the then mainstream kitchens; others had never worked in a kitchen but were desperate to. Most (like myself) were 'self-taught', but all had that essential passion for eating real food and, regardless of their ability, all of them were necessarily dropped into the thick of it – the kitchen had space for only two cooks, remember. Nearly all the cooks that have passed through the Eagle's kitchen are still cooking, and an awful lot of them have their own establishments. It is their influences that have shaped the kitchen's repertoire. The maxim, 'Big Flavours and Rough Edges', is paraphrased from an early review in *The Times*. Jonathan Meades was, I suspect, qualifying an otherwise favourable column, but I've always taken the description to be flattering and perfectly apt. The kitchen still has space for only two, the menu still changes every day, and the Eagle is still a pub that happens to serve grilled scallops instead of microwaved scampi.

I'd like to dedicate this book to all who have worked at the Eagle P.H.; to the customers who have been keen but unwitting guinea pigs whilst we were learning lots; and to my mother, who taught me what good food should be in the middle of nowhere in colonial Mozambique.

David Eyre
Introduction to the original Eagle recipe collection, *Big Flavours & Rough Edges*, published July 2000

Over the years, a host of enthusiastic, intelligent young chefs have squeezed into our tiny kitchen. Two at a time, they have catered for as many as 120 customers in a busy lunchtime session. So many new kitchens have been conceived here that David calls it a 'stud farm for chefs', a metaphor which also hints at some of the fun we've had cooking the food! These recipes should help you to join in the fun. Of course, not all of them could make a contribution to the book, but they all helped to make the Eagle the special place that it is. These are the ones who took it a little bit further, and opened places of their own:

Amanda Pritchett was first off the mark with the Lansdowne in Primrose Hill. The Sam Clarks met in the Eagle kitchen and later established the fabulous Moro, just up the road in Exmouth Market, and we spawned another competitor when Jake Hodges left to establish Cigala in Bloomsbury. Margot Henderson set up the French House Dining Room with husband, Fergus, and we all know where that led to. She now runs the Rochelle Canteen and caters for arty events all over the world. After seven years, David left to open Eyre Bros with his brother Rob in Shoreditch, and I moved into The Fox, around the corner. Trish Hilferty and Harry Lester set up the kitchen there. Amanda Pritchett has now taken it over. George Manners asked us for a job in 1996 to learn how it was done and two years later, set up a chain of West London Gastropubs starting with The Atlas near Earls Court. Harry Lester popped up again with the hugely influential Anchor and Hope where Trish Hilferty is now co-Head Chef. Harry now runs a charming hotel in the Auvergne: 'Auberge de Chassignolles'. Finally, after a stint of writing cookbooks and foodie journalism, Tom Norrington-Davies is back where he belongs – manning the stoves at Great Queen Street! There he is Head Chef and partner. He helped enormously with the publication of this new edition, as did Trish, who cooked and styled all of the food.

Mike Belben
June 2009

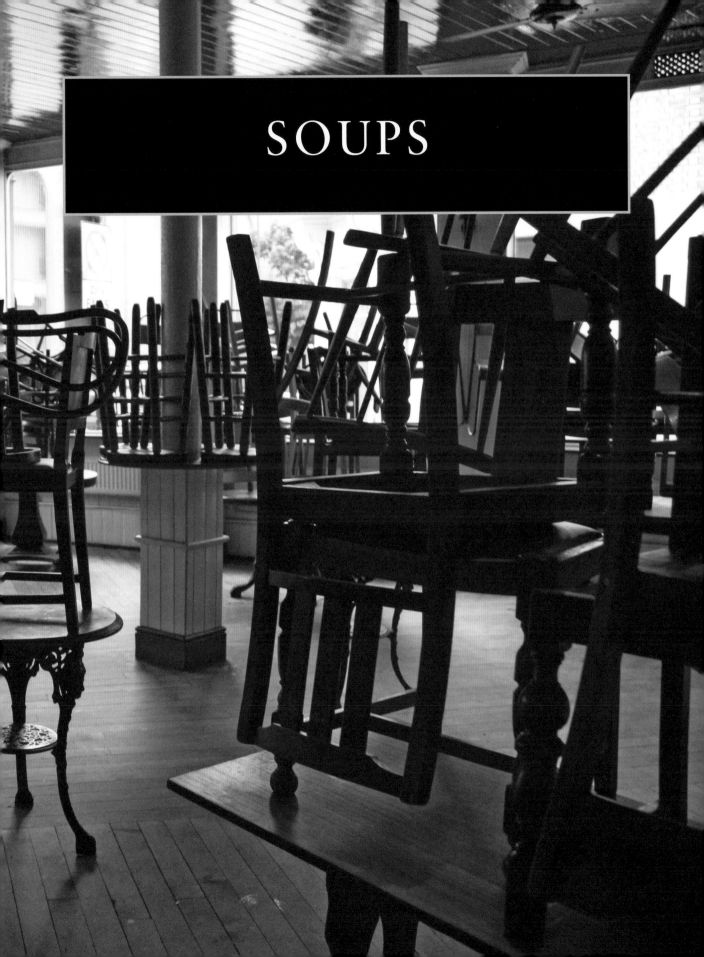

SOUPS

ABOUT OUR SOUPS

If you've ever eaten it, you will know that there is absolutely nothing subtle about *sopa de pedra*: northern Portugal's answer to Italian minestrones or French and Spanish pottages. The perplexing translation of its name is 'stone soup', the story being that a penniless and hungry traveler arrives in a village and announces that he is able to conjure the tastiest soup for the whole village from nothing more than a large pan of water and a stone. These are provided and, whilst solemnly stirring the pot, he suggests that though the soup will be quite delicious it would be improved with cabbage and a little chorizo sausage. These are eagerly fetched and a little later he repeats the suggestion that perhaps an onion and some beans would be a small improvement – and so on until he has a fine catch-all dish. Improvisatory recipes like this have always been the inspiration behind soups at the Eagle. Some of them are thick and heartwarming, the kind of soups that make damp winters seem not so very bad. Others are brothy and restorative. In the summer, they might be chilled. One thing unites all of them: in a pub that celebrates one-plate eating, soup should provide an entire meal in a bowl.

PORTUGUESE 'STONE' SOUP
SOPA DE PEDRA DAVID EYRE

Within reason, *sopa de pedra* can include any cured pork and vegetables, so this recipe may be modified as you wish. However, it should always include chorizo, cabbage and beans. It is also one of those composite dishes that benefit from being made the previous day, but be sure to cool it down as rapidly as you can; warm beans love to ferment, given the chance.

250g/9oz red beans, such as kidney beans,
  soaked overnight in cold water
200g/7oz piece of smoked bacon or pancetta
a gammon hock or a raw ham end
  (most delicatessens are happy to sell these
  cheaply)
2 chorizo sausages
1 black pudding – if you can find the
  Portuguese morçela *or the Spanish*
  morcilla, *all the better*
2 onions, chopped
2 small turnips, chopped
2 carrots, chopped
400g/14oz waxy potatoes, cut into spoon-
  sized pieces
3 garlic cloves, sliced
2 tablespoons tomato purée
2 tablespoons massa de pimentão *(red*
  pepper purée – not essential but a good
  thing to have; Turkish grocers stock a
  similar product, or use puréed roasted red
  pepper)
100ml/3½fl oz olive oil
the darker leaves from a smallish Savoy
  cabbage, shredded
a bay leaf or two and some thyme and
  parsley
salt and freshly ground black pepper

Drain the red beans, put them in a large pan and cover with water. Bring to the boil and cook vigorously for 10 minutes. Drain and rinse off any scum from the beans. Return to the pan with 2 litres/3½ pints water, the smoked bacon, gammon hock, chorizo sausages and black pudding. Simmer steadily until the beans are nearly cooked. Remove the meat and cut it into pieces.

In a separate pan, fry the chopped vegetables, garlic, tomato purée and red pepper purée in the olive oil for a few minutes, until softened a little. While they are still bright, add the vegetables to the beans with the meat, cabbage and herbs. Cook for a further 20 minutes or until the beans are soft, then correct the seasoning. Serve with bread.

PEAS WITH CHORIZO AND POACHED EGG DAVID EYRE

A simple Portuguese recipe that could be considered a soup, though when served with a poached egg it is elevated to a cosy supper dish. I nearly always use frozen tiny petit pois, unless very fresh young peas are available. Similarly, Spanish chorizo is often more readily available than my preferred Portuguese *chouriço*, which is generally drier, coarser and fattier.

1 large white onion, chopped
3 tablespoons olive oil or 2 tablespoons
*   good-quality lard*
2 garlic cloves, finely chopped
3 tablespoons chopped flat-leaf parsley
150g/5oz chorizo, sliced
800g/1 1/3 lb small peas, very fresh or good
*   quality frozen*
1 litre/1 3/4 pints light meat stock or water
4 very fresh 'real' (i.e. organic) eggs
salt and freshly ground black pepper

Gently fry the onion in the olive oil or lard until transparent, then add the garlic and parsley. At the same time cook the sliced chorizo in a dry pan over a very low flame to melt some of the fat. Drain the chorizo and add to the onion with the peas and stock or water. Cook for about 10 minutes, then purée a cupful of the peas in a blender to thicken the soup. Season generously with black pepper – you may not need any salt, depending on the saltiness of the sausage.

When ready to serve, poach an egg for each person in a saucepan with a teaspoon of vinegar in the normal manner. Ladle the soup into bowls and place an egg on each portion.

RED ONION AND RED WINE SOUP WITH PARMESAN BRUSCHETTA

GEORGE MANNERS

Northern Italian in origin, this is a satisfying and warming winter soup – thick and juicy, with tangy sweetness.

1 bottle of red wine
4 cloves
4 bay leaves
a few sprigs of thyme, plus extra to garnish
50g/2oz butter
4 tablespoons olive oil
12 red onions, sliced
4 garlic cloves, chopped
2 teaspoons tomato purée
500ml/18fl oz vegetable stock
2 tablespoons balsamic vinegar
1 teaspoon ground cinnamon

For the Parmesan bruschetta
6 slices country-style bread
2 garlic cloves, peeled and halved
extra virgin olive oil
freshly grated Parmesan cheese

Pour the wine into a casserole, add the cloves, bay leaves and half the thyme and boil over a high heat until reduced by half. Strain, reserving the liquid. In the same casserole, melt the butter in the olive oil, then add the red onions and garlic. Cook gently over a medium heat until sweet and tender, stirring from time to time – this will take at least half an hour. Add the reduced wine, tomato purée, vegetable stock and the remaining thyme, and cook at a gentle simmer for half an hour. Stir in the balsamic vinegar and cinnamon and leave the mixture to simmer for a further 15 minutes. Check the seasoning.

To make the bruschetta, toast the bread on a griddle or in a dry heavy-based frying pan, then rub with the garlic and drizzle over some extra virgin olive oil. Sprinkle with a liberal layer of grated Parmesan.

Put a piece of Parmesan bruschetta in each soup bowl and pour over the soup. Serve garnished with a couple of sprigs of thyme.

ROOT VEGETABLE SOUP
WITH GREENS TOM NORRINGTON-DAVIES

Simple broths thickened with potato and stale bread are known in Italy as *pancotto*. The more root vegetables you add the better, but potatoes and onions alone will do the trick. The greens, too, are open to interpretation. In the winter months choose hardy brassica, like Savoy cabbage or Brussels sprout tops. In the summer use young spinach, rocket or even herbs. Chervil and flat-leaf parsley work best.

You do not need stock for this soup – sweating several vegetables together with oil and a little water will give you all the flavour you need. But feel free to use chicken or vegetable stock if you want to.

3 tablespoons olive oil
3 onions, chopped
2 garlic cloves, peeled and slightly crushed
2 large floury potatoes (baking potatoes or 'whites'), peeled and roughly diced
about 500g/1lb 2oz vegetables, such as turnips, parsnips, celeriac, fennel and leeks (the more anaemic looking the better, so avoid pumpkin, beetroot and carrots), peeled and diced
a mugful of water
about 100g/4oz stale, rustic-style bread, such as sourdough or ciabatta, with the crusts removed
3 generous handfuls of chopped greens
salt and freshly ground black pepper
extra virgin olive oil, to serve

Gently heat the oil in a large, heavy-bottomed pan, add the onions and garlic and fry until soft, without browning. Add the potatoes and other vegetables, plus a couple of pinches of salt and about half the mug of water. Stir thoroughly and cover. Leave to simmer gently for about 20 minutes or until all the vegetables are tender. Add the stale bread and a little more water. When the bread has gone soft, gently mash everything together and start to add more water until you have the consistency you want. Remember it should be broth-like enough to be able to cook the greens in. Season to taste with salt and pepper.

Bring the soup to a simmer again and add the greens. If using cabbage, the soup will need another 5 minutes' simmering. If using herbs or rocket, serve immediately. Garnish each bowlful with a drizzle of extra virgin olive oil.

VARIATIONS

• Meat eaters can include bacon in the soup. It should be added to the pot with the onions and garlic.
• If there is Parmesan or pecorino in the fridge, grate some and put it in a bowl on the table when you serve the soup.
• *Pancotto* made with rocket is traditionally garnished with crushed dried chillies as well as with the extra virgin olive oil.

GREENS AND POTATO SOUP WITH CHOURIÇO CALDO VERDE DAVID EYRE

You'll find this on every Portuguese menu and, like all potato-based soups, it is really easy to make, needing only an onion or so as the aromatic element. If the potatoes are flavourful, stock is unnecessary. Be sure to use floury rather than waxy varieties of potatos otherwise the result will be glutinous; those labelled as baking potatoes are ideal.

1 large onion, finely chopped
2 large garlic cloves, finely chopped
100ml/3¹/₂fl oz good olive oil, plus extra to
 serve
4 or 5 large baking potatoes, peeled and
 diced
200g/7oz spicy Portuguese chouriço sausage
 (the dried type are best)
800g/1³/₄lb dark spring greens (weight after
 the stalks have been removed)
salt and freshly ground black pepper

Gently cook the onion and garlic in the olive oil for a few minutes until softened. Add the potatoes and pour over enough water to cover. Bring to the boil and simmer until the potatoes begin to collapse. Mash the potatoes in the pot and then thin the soup with 1 litre/1³/₄ pints water.

Meanwhile thinly slice the chouriço and put it into a cold, greased heavy frying pan. Fry over a low heat until the chouriço is crisp and most of the fat has melted. Drain on kitchen paper and add to the soup. Season with salt and pepper to taste and keep warm.

Shred the greens into fine filaments. The best way to do this is to take 6 or so de-stalked leaves, roll them into a tight 'cigar' and then cut it into thin strips with a large, sharp knife. A julienne disc on a good processor may work if the cigar fills the feed tube tightly. In any case, aim for the sliced to be 1–2mm/¹/₁₂ inch wide.

When almost ready to serve, throw the cabbage into the soup and simmer until it is bright green. Garnish each bowl with a drizzle of olive oil.

FLORENTINE PEA SOUP CARABACCIA

DAVID EYRE

SERVES 6

This is an absolute favourite springtime soup, making the best use of the starchiness of fresh peas (although I confess that I'm happy to make an ersatz version at any time of the year using frozen peas). Considered by the Tuscans to be primarily an onion soup, Carabaccia dates from the Renaissance, when it was sweetened with cinnamon and almonds. It is sometimes served with a poached egg on top.

100ml/3^1/$_2$fl oz olive oil, plus extra for the
   bread
3 large onions, chopped
3 celery sticks, chopped
1 carrot, finely chopped
1 garlic clove, finely chopped
500g/1lb 2oz freshly podded peas (about
   1.2kg/2^3/$_4$lb unpodded weight)
1 litre/1^3/$_4$ pints light chicken or vegetable
   stock
6 slices of day-old white, country-style
   bread, such as pugliese or pain de
   campagne
salt and freshly ground black pepper
freshly grated Parmesan cheese, to serve

Heat the oil in a large pan, add the onions, celery, carrot, garlic and some salt and pepper, then cover and cook over a low heat for about an hour, until the vegetables become a very soft mush. Add the peas and a little of the stock and simmer for 10 minutes, or until the peas are tender. Purée half of the soup in a blender. Return it to the pan with the rest of the stock and reheat.

Toast the bread and oil it generously. Place a slice in each soup bowl, pour over the soup and serve with grated Parmesan.

BLACK BEAN SOUP

GEORGE MANNERS

This was adapted from the black beans that are prevalent in San Francisco's *taquerias*, where some of the best Mexican food is to be found. They are the mainstay of any burritos worth their salt. The soup is as nourishing as it is simple to make, and hearty sustenance when faced, as I regularly am, with an empty fridge at home.

250g/9oz black beans or Spanish frijoles negras, soaked overnight in cold water
about 1.5 litres/2¹/₂ pints light vegetable stock or water
2 white onions, chopped
2 garlic cloves, chopped
1 red chilli, seeded and finely chopped
1 celery stick, chopped
3 tablespoons sunflower oil
1 tablespoon cumin seeds, lightly toasted in a dry frying pan
400g/14oz tin tomatoes, drained and squeezed
a fairly big bunch of coriander, coarsely chopped
a pinch of sugar
150ml/¹/₄ pint soured cream (or double cream whipped with a squeeze of lemon juice)
salt and freshly ground black pepper

Drain the black beans, cover with fresh water, then bring to the boil and drain again. Return to the pan, cover with the stock or water and bring to a simmer. Make sure there is plenty of liquid as the beans will swell and eventually release their starch into the soup, thus thickening the liquid.

In a separate pan, fry the onions, garlic, chilli and celery in the oil until translucent. Add the toasted cumin seeds and cook for a few minutes to blend the flavours. Then add the tomatoes and most of the coriander. Cook down and then stir all the vegetables into the beans as they begin to soften. Leave to simmer for half an hour or so, to allow all the flavours to blend. Season with the sugar and some salt. You may not need any pepper because of the chilli. Serve garnished with a dollop of soured cream and the remaining coriander.

NOTE

This recipe may be served as a wonderful accompaniment to cooked meat if you use much less stock and allow the mixture to thicken.

PORTUGUESE CHICKEN BROTH WITH RICE, MINT AND LEMON CANJA

DAVID EYRE

This is almost Portugal's national dish, at least in the down-home section. It's a kind of always-available-even-if-too-late-for-lunch restaurant dish. Anyway, this is not an apology; it's the best of all chicken soups, with proven restorative qualities.

2 large chicken breasts, washed
rind of 1 lemon (use a potato peeler)
a dozen mint leaves, chopped
200g/7oz rice (or rice-shaped pasta)
juice of 1 lemon
salt and freshly ground black pepper

For the stock
1 boiling chicken or 1kg/2¼lb chicken wings
  or drumsticks, washed
a carrot, an onion, 2 celery sticks –
  all roughly chopped
some bay leaves and peppercorns
some parsley and mint stalks

For the stock, put all the ingredients in a large pan, cover with about 3 litres/5 pints cold water and bring to a gentle simmer. Simmer for an hour but don't let it boil, even for a minute, or the fat will emulsify and the stock become cloudy – the aim is an infusion of the chicken and aromatics. Strain the stock and skim the fat from the surface. If you are making it in advance, you can chill the stock and then simply lift off the solidified fat.

Return the stock to the clean pan and reheat it, then poach the chicken breasts in it with the lemon rind and chopped mint. Remove the chicken breasts when they are cooked and slice into thin strips. Return them to the pan with the rice (or tiny pasta) and the lemon juice. When the rice is cooked, season the soup – you may need more lemon juice – and serve immediately.

BLACK MUSHROOM SOUP

DAVID EYRE

This has the appearance of a broth or *consommé*. The addition of tiny soup pasta makes it more substantial but I sometimes prefer to serve it over a large slice of grilled bread.

25g/1oz dried ceps (or more if you want deeper notes to the end result)
1 large onion, finely chopped
1 large leek, finely chopped
1 celery stick, finely chopped
2 garlic cloves, sliced
800g/1³/₄lb field mushrooms, finely sliced
about 20 sage leaves, chopped
100ml/3¹/₂fl oz olive oil
1 litre/1³/₄ pints water or chicken stock
200g/7 oz small soup pasta, such as ditalini, mezzi tubetti or conchigliette
a couple of mint sprigs, chopped just before you add them to the pan
juice of 1 or more lemons, to taste
salt and freshly ground black pepper

To serve
freshly grated Parmesan cheese / grilled country-style bread rubbed with garlic (optional)

Soak the dried ceps in 1 litre/1³/₄ pints hot water for 30 minutes. In a covered pan, gently cook the onion, leek, celery, garlic, field mushrooms and sage in the olive oil with some salt. When the mushrooms have steamed themselves to an almost black colour, add the ceps, together with their strained soaking liquor and the water or chicken stock. Simmer gently for 30 minutes. Meanwhile, cook the soup pasta separately until *al dente*, then drain.

Check the seasoning of the soup, stir in the mint and add the lemon juice to taste. Divide the pasta between individual bowls, pour the soup on top and serve with Parmesan and grilled garlic-rubbed bread, if using

SPICY MUSSEL SOUP

ED MOTTERSHAW

SERVES 4–6

A wonderfully fragrant soup that is ideal as a light lunch or supper dish. The long, slow cooking time results in an intense combination of classic Mediterranean flavours.

5 tablespoons olive oil
3 red chillies (de-seeded if you don't want the heat), chopped
6 garlic cloves, finely chopped
6 anchovy fillets, drained and chopped
3 x 400g cans tomatoes, drained and juice discarded
1kg live mussels, scrubbed, rinsed and beards removed
100ml/3¹/₂fl oz white wine
salt and freshly ground black pepper
bruschetta, to serve

In a large pan, heat 2 tablespoons of the olive oil over a medium heat and fry the chopped chilli, garlic and anchovies, but do not allow them to brown. Add the tomatoes to the pan, cover but leave the lid ajar, reduce the heat and leave to cook gently.

Discard any mussels that do not close when tapped. Put them in a large pan with the remaining olive oil, wine and 100ml/3¹/₂fl oz water, cover and bring to the boil. Steam the mussels for 5–6 minutes, until the shells open. Drain, reserving the cooking liquor and discard any shells that haven't opened. Set the cooked mussels to one side.

Add the mussel cooking liquor to the tomatoes and break them up using a potato masher. Cook over a low heat, for about 1¹/₂ hours – until the tomatoes and oil separate.

Season the soup to taste. Return the cooked mussels to the pan and heat them through until piping hot. Serve the soup with bruschetta.

ANDALUCIAN GARLIC SOUP WITH SOFT-BOILED EGG SOPA AL AJILLIO

TRISH HILFERTY

This is one of the many recipes I was taught by Adam Robinson while working at the Brackenbury restaurant in West London. Like much of his food, it is simple and really tasty. Serve with chilled dry sherry.

a day-old loaf of heavy white bread (Italian, sourdough or even ciabatta)
2 heads of garlic, separated into cloves, unpeeled
150ml/¹/₄ pint olive oil
2.5 litres/4¹/₂ pints good chicken stock
a big pinch of saffron
6 free-range eggs, soft-boiled and shelled
sea salt and freshly ground black pepper

Trim the hard crusts off the loaf and separate the bread into chunks. Put the bread and garlic cloves on a baking tray and douse with the olive oil, then season with sea salt and a grinding of black pepper. Cover with a lid or foil and bake slowly in an oven preheated to 150°C/gas mark 2, until the bread is golden and has soaked up the oil, and the garlic is soft. This may take about 30–40 minutes. Leave to cool, then squeeze the garlic from its skin and purée in a blender or food processor with the bread to make crumbs.

Bring the stock to the boil with the saffron. Add the crumbs and bring the mixture back to a simmer. Adjust the seasoning. Place a soft-boiled egg in each warm serving bowl and pour the soup over.

GAZPACHO ANDALUZ
CARLOS VARGAS

Gazpacho, meaning cold soup, comes from Andalucia. This refreshing soup was historically made for agricultural workers during the hot summer months. Traditionally it was prepared using a pestle and mortar but these days you can save a lot of time with a food processor. There are as many gazpacho recipes as there are people who make it. They all have their own secrets.

To skin the tomatoes, pour boiling water over them and drain after 30 seconds. The skin should then come off easily.

3 garlic cloves, chopped
500g/1lb 2oz ripe tomatoes, skinned and
*   seeded*
2 green peppers, chopped
2 small cucumbers, peeled and chopped
250g/9oz stale white country-style bread,
*   torn into small chunks*
250ml/8fl oz olive oil
3 tablespoons sherry vinegar
1.5 litres/2¹⁄₂ pints water and ice, mixed
salt

Pulse the garlic, tomatoes, peppers and cucumbers in a food processor until well mixed. Strain the mixture through a sieve to remove the pepper skins. Stir in the bread, olive oil, vinegar, iced water and salt to taste; the bread will soften and dissolve in the liquid. Chill before serving.

CHICKPEA STEW (OR IS IT A SOUP?)

POTAJE DE GARBANZOS CARLOS VARGAS

SERVES 6–8

A *potaje* is one of the most popular poor foods in Spain. By 'poor', I mean that it is made from cheap, storecupboard ingredients. *Potaje* is a word used mainly by Andalucians. If you go further north, a similar dish would be called *cocido* or even *olla*, which means simply a pot. *Potaje* contains stock with meat or fish and either dried beans or chickpeas. It doesn't need to be carefully watched and tended, making it popular with busy housewives. The final point about *potaje* is that it tastes even better the day after it is made. The meat can be left out if you prefer.

150ml/¼ pint olive oil
2 bay leaves
500g/1lb 2oz chickpeas, soaked overnight in
  plenty of cold water
a piece of Serrano ham fat and trimmings,
  or similar
2 fresh chorizos, sliced
50g/2oz pancetta, chopped
50g/2oz white country-style bread, cut or
  torn into small pieces
4 tablespoons chopped flat-leaf parsley
1 egg, hard-boiled and chopped
6 garlic cloves, unpeeled
300g/11oz potatoes, peeled and chopped
300g/11oz spinach or Swiss chard, roughly
  chopped
salt

In a large pan, bring 2 litres/3½ pints of water to the boil with 3 tablespoons of the olive oil and the bay leaves. Drain the soaked chickpeas and add them to the boiling water with the ham fat and trimmings, chorizo and pancetta. Simmer for about half an hour.

In another pan, gently fry the bread, parsley and garlic in the remaining olive oil until lightly coloured. Add this to the chickpeas with the hard-boiled egg, potatoes and spinach or Swiss chard. Cook for about 40 minutes – 1 hour, until the chickpeas are soft. Take out the ham and roughly mash the stew to break up some of the chickpeas and the garlic. Taste and adjust the seasoning. You might be surprised at how much salt you need to add. Add a little, stir, leave to rest for a few minutes then taste again.

COLD ROAST AUBERGINE SOUP WITH YOGHURT TOM NORRINGTON-DAVIES

SERVES 8

The flavour of this soup will vary slightly according to how you roast the aubergines. Charring them over a gas flame or grill gives a smoky edge, whereas roasting them in a hot oven results in a rich, slightly buttery taste.

4 large aubergines, pricked all over
2 red peppers
2 tablespoons olive oil
3 onions, finely chopped
3 garlic cloves, finely chopped
1 teaspoon paprika
500ml/18fl oz Greek-style yoghurt
about 1 litre/1³/₄ pints vegetable stock
  or water
salt and freshly ground black pepper

Char the aubergines over a gas flame for 10–15 minutes, turning them occasionally, until they are blackened and 'collapsed' and feel very soft. Alternatively, brush them with a little olive oil, sprinkle with salt and put them in the oven at full blast for about 30 minutes, until very soft. Roast the red peppers at the same time, until charred all over. Put the aubergines and peppers in a large bowl and cover with a plate – this creates steam which helps to loosen the skin. Leave for at least half an hour.

Meanwhile, gently heat the olive oil in a large pan and add the onions and garlic. Cover and sweat very gently, without letting them brown, for about 30 minutes, until soft and translucent. Halfway through this time, stir in the paprika.

Now remove the skin from the aubergines – they may well fall apart on you as you do this, which is a good thing. It is tempting to skin them under a tap but try not to, as you will lose some flavour. Don't worry if there are little bits of charred skin on the flesh; they will disappear when you purée them. Strip the skin off the roasted peppers too, discard the seeds, then finely chop the flesh and toss with a little olive oil and salt. Set aside.

Remove the onions and garlic from the heat and stir in the aubergine flesh, then purée to a smooth paste in a blender. Transfer to a bowl. Once the paste has cooled down (it doesn't need to be stone cold), add the yoghurt and stir until it is fully incorporated. Now dilute the mixture by adding cold stock or water; keep it nice and thick, so that the roasted peppers will float on top. Season to taste with salt and pepper. To serve, pour into individual bowls and garnish with the roasted peppers.

PASTA & BEAN SOUP
MINESTRA PASTA E FAGIOLI RUTH QUINLAN

Minestrone is literally a 'big soup', which uses lots of different ingredients and epitomises earthy, meal-in-a-bowl eating. If you don't intend to eat the soup straight away, or if you are making enough for more than one meal, don't cook the pasta in the soup or it will eventually become soggy. Instead, cook it separately just before you eat and add it to the soup as you serve it.

500g/1lb 2oz dried beans, such as borlotti or cannellini, soaked overnight in cold water
4 tablespoons olive oil
250g/9oz pancetta, chopped
2 medium onions, chopped
2 carrots, chopped
2 garlic cloves, finely chopped
3 celery sticks, chopped
2 branches of flat-leaf parsley
a sprig of rosemary
2 sprigs of oregano
400g/14oz tinned tomatoes, drained and chopped
250g/9oz pasta, such as ditali or macaroni, or noodles snapped into short lengths
100ml/3½fl oz extra virgin olive oil, warmed
salt and freshly ground black pepper
freshly grated Parmesan cheese, to serve

Drain the soaked beans, put them in a large pot and cover with fresh water. Bring to the boil and boil for 10 minutes (don't add any salt or the beans will become too tough). Drain the beans and wash any scum from them.

Heat the olive oil in a large pan, add the pancetta, onions, carrots, garlic, celery, parsley, rosemary and oregano and cook gently until the vegetables are softened. Add the tomatoes and the drained beans, then pour in enough water to cover the pot contents by 5cm/2 inches. Cook steadily with the lid on for 1–2 hours depending on how fresh the beans are, until they are soft but still whole. Remove a couple of ladlefuls of beans and purée them; stir them back into the pot to thicken it. Now add salt and pepper to taste and fish out the herb branches. Add the pasta to the soup and cook until tender, then turn off the heat and stir in the warm olive oil. Serve with Parmesan cheese and bread.

PORK AND BEAN SOUP

ED MOTTERSHAW

SERVES 6

A hearty Spanish-style main course soup. Serve with lots of crusty bread to make sure you mop up the very last mouthful.

400g/14oz dried butter beans
1 x medium-sized ham hock
200g/7oz pork belly
200g/7oz pancetta
1 bouquet garni
3 onions, sliced
12 garlic cloves, finely chopped
100g/3½oz chorizo sausage
½ teaspoon paprika
salt and freshly ground black pepper
small handful of chopped parsley, to garnish

Soak the butter beans in cold water for 8 hours or overnight.

Drain the soaked beans and rinse them thoroughly in cold running water. Place the beans in a large pan with the ham hock, pork belly and pancetta. Add enough cold water to the pan to cover the meat and beans by 5cm/2 inches. Add the bouquet garni to the pan and bring to the boil. Turn the heat down to a slow simmer, cover and cook for 1 hour, removing any scum that forms on the surface.

After an hour, add the onions, garlic, chorizo sausage and paprika to the pan. Cook for 1–1½ hours or until the meat and beans are cooked and tender.

Use a slotted spoon to remove the meat from the pan. Chop the meat and chorizo into bite-size pieces, return it to the pan and heat through until it is piping hot. Season the soup with salt and pepper and sprinkle the parsley over just before serving.

SALADS

GREEK SALAD
DAVID EYRE

A WORD ON SALADS

To understand the robust salads that are eaten all around the Mediterranean, a little historical context is needed. The modern day word descends from 'salata', meaning 'salted'. The focus of such a dish is therefore not the leaves, but any number of preserved or pickled ingredients. The French salade niçoise on page 47 is exemplary, with its jumble of confited tuna, briny capers and salted anchovies. The Greek mix of feta and olives in the recipe on this page is a near relative. Whenever we throw a salad together at the Eagle we try and bring a little of this Mediterranean spirit to Farringdon Road.

Unlike the bottle of Metaxa brought home from your holiday in the islands, a Greek salad travels well if reserved for the hottest of summer days. I make a variation for balmier days that uses green beans, fresh broad beans and peas in place of cucumber, and fresh coriander and mint in place of oregano and caper berries.

12 ripe tomatoes, quartered
2 cucumbers, partially peeled, halved down
    their length and then sliced
1 large red onion, very finely sliced
250–300g /9–11oz ewe's milk feta cheese,
    broken into large pieces
150ml/$^1/_4$ pint fruity olive oil
juice of 2 lemons
1 tablespoon dried or fresh oregano
a handful of kalamata olives
a dozen caper berries, washed of their brine
    or vinegar

Divide the tomatoes, cucumbers and onion between 4 plates and place the feta on top. Whisk the olive oil, lemon juice and oregano together and use to dress the salad. Garnish with the olives and caper berries.

CUT SEARED BEEF SALAD
TAGLIATA **DAVID EYRE**

I have modified the original Italian dish with the addition of fresh tarragon – tarragon and beef being a favourite combo of mine. I also prefer to cut the steak after, not before, cooking.

100g/4oz waxy new potatoes, such as
  Charlotte, La Ratte, Belle de Fontenay,
  Jersey Royals or Pink Fir Apple
2 x 225g/8oz steaks – forerib fillet (ribeye),
  sirloin or fillet
100g/4oz rocket
1 tablespoon good Modena balsamic
  vinegar, but don't spend silly amounts
3 tablespoons really good olive oil
1 tablespoon chopped tarragon
coarse sea salt or Maldon salt and freshly
  ground black pepper

Boil the potatoes in salted water until tender, then drain. Grill or fry the steaks rare (see About Grillling Meat, page 130) and then leave to rest on a warm plate. Cut the potatoes into pieces. Divide the rocket and potatoes between 2 serving plates. Make a dressing with the vinegar, oil, tarragon and some sea salt and pepper. Cut the steaks into thin strips, mix with the dressing and then scatter them over the salad.

ROAST PUMPKIN AND RED ONION SALAD JORGE CARDOSO

SERVES 4

This dish has fabulous colours. The salty Parmesan makes a great contrast to the sweet vegetables. These quantities are enough for a first course or light meal. It also goes well with grilled fish. The salad is served at room temperature, so you need to allow a couple of hours for the roasted vegetables to cool.

6 tablespoons olive oil
6 red onions, peeled and halved
100ml/3½fl oz red wine
2 tablespoons balsamic vinegar
3 sprigs of thyme
½–1 small pumpkin (or you could use 2 butternut squash)
2 handfuls of rocket (about 200g/7oz)
a block of Parmesan cheese (at least 50g/2oz)
salt and freshly ground black pepper

Put half the oil into a deep heatproof baking dish or heavy-duty roasting tin on a high heat. Add the onions, stirring them to distribute the oil. Add the red wine, balsamic vinegar and some salt and pepper. The balsamic vinegar intensifies the colour of the onions and caramelises them. Strip the leaves from the thyme and throw them in. When the mixture is bubbling away, cover tightly with foil, transfer to an oven preheated to 200°C/gas mark 6 and bake for 30 minutes. Remove the foil and bake for a further 10 minutes, until tender.

Cut the pumpkin into segments, following its natural creases; peel, and scrape out the seeds. Place the segments on a baking tray, drizzle with the remaining olive oil and season with salt and pepper. Roast at 200°C/gas mark 6 for 20–30 minutes or until brown at the edges and soft to the point of a sharp knife.

Leave the vegetables to cool to room temperature, then toss them with the rocket, using the juices from the red onion as a dressing. Top with shavings of the Parmesan.

BAKED AUBERGINES STUFFED WITH TOMATOES IMAM BAYELDI TRISH HILFERTY

SERVES 6

This is a classic Turkish dish. The name means 'the Imam fainted', the story being that the Imam, or clergyman, swooned with joy when his wife presented it to him. Serve with a green salad dressed with tahini and lemon.

6 aubergines, halved lengthways
4 red onions, sliced
2 garlic cloves, sliced
150ml/¼ pint olive oil, plus a little extra for
   drizzling
1 teaspoon cumin seeds
1 teaspoon dried mint
400g/14oz tomatoes, diced
2 bay leaves
a small bunch of coriander, stems chopped,
   leaves reserved
1 lemon
salt and freshly ground black pepper

Score the flesh of the aubergines, then scoop it out with a spoon, being careful not to tear the skin. Dice the flesh, salt it lightly and set aside in a colander to drain. Salt the shells and leave them upside down to drain for 30 minutes. Wash and pat dry.

Sweat the onion and garlic in 100ml/3½fl oz of the olive oil or until they are soft. Stir in the cumin seeds and mint and cook for 1 minute. Add the tomatoes and bay and cook for 5 minutes, then transfer the mixture to a bowl.

Rinse and dry the aubergine flesh. Heat the remaining olive oil and sauté the aubergine until soft and light brown, then add to the tomato mixture. Adjust the seasoning and mix in the chopped coriander stems.

Spoon the filling into the aubergine shells and fit them into an oiled baking dish in a single layer. Squeeze over the lemon juice and pour in enough water to come halfway up the side of the aubergines. Drizzle over a little more oil, then bake in an oven preheated to 180°C/gas mark 4 for 30–40 minutes, until the shells are soft. Leave to cool. Serve at room temperature, strewn with coriander leaves.

SALAD NIÇOISE
DAVID EYRE

So much has been said about how to make the true *salade niçoise* that I know I'm courting complaint just by providing a recipe. Some say no tuna, some no anchovies, some say nothing cooked, and so on. Still, there is no finer lunch or more perfectly balanced plate of food. This, then, is my *vrai salade niçoise*.
I prefer to use Spanish yellowfin or *bonito* tuna in olive oil – skipjack and albacore are best left for the cat. Tinned tuna in brine is horrid.

75g/3oz green beans (any type)
250g/9oz new potatoes
4 eggs
100ml/3½fl oz olive oil
1 tablespoon lemon juice
1 smallish Cos lettuce
75g/3oz fresh or dried butter beans, broad beans, white haricots or whatever is around, cooked
6 ripe tomatoes, cut into eighths
250g/9oz tinned tuna in oil, drained
2 tablespoons salted capers, rinsed several times and then left to soak until no longer salty
100g/4oz small, tasty olives
8 cured anchovy fillets (see page 115)
freshly ground black pepper

Cook the green beans, uncovered, in boiling salted water until just tender, then drain and immediately plunge into cold water to set their colour. Drain again. Cook the potatoes until tender, then drain. Boil the eggs for just 5 minutes so that the yolks are still slightly 'greasy'. Cool in cold water, then shell and halve them.

Whisk the oil and lemon together with some black pepper. Toss the lettuce leaves with a little of this dressing. Mix the green beans, potatoes, cooked fresh or dried beans, tomatoes and a third of the tuna with more dressing. Divide the lettuce between 4 large plates or shallow bowls and then pile the vegetables on top. Toss the remaining tuna and the capers, olives and anchovy fillets with the remaining dressing and divide them, with the halved eggs, between the plates.

GRILLED CHICKEN SALAD WITH TRUFFLE OIL POLA WICKHAM

SERVES 4

You will need four long wooden skewers for this recipe. Soak them in water for half an hour or so before use, to prevent them burning on the grill.

4 skinless, boneless free-range chicken
   breasts, each cut into 4
5 tablespoons olive oil
2 large red peppers
450g/1lb new potatoes
125g/4$\frac{1}{2}$oz finely sliced coppa di Parma (or
   pancetta coppata or pancetta stesa)
about 200g/7oz rocket
5 teaspoons capers, soaked in cold water for
   30 minutes and then squeezed
2 tablespoons black kalamata or Niçoise
   olives, pitted
1 tablespoon lemon juice
4–5 tablespoons white truffle oil
salt and freshly ground black pepper
lemon wedges, to serve

Thread the chicken pieces on to the soaked skewers, rub with 3 tablespoons of the olive oil and season with salt and pepper.

Put the red peppers under a hot grill, turning them occasionally, so that the skin starts to blister and blacken all over. When they are charred, put them into a bowl and leave to cool for about half an hour. Remove the skin, which should now come off easily, and cut the peppers into strips.

Put the potatoes in a pan and cover with cold water. Add a decent pinch of salt, bring to the boil and cook for about 20 minutes or until they are tender. Drain them, cut each in half and season with a little salt while they are still hot.

Grill the chicken skewers on a chargrill pan or under an overhead grill for about 15 minutes, until cooked through. Meanwhile, take the rind off the *coppa* if necessary and cut each slice in half. Tear the rocket into pieces and put it in a large mixing bowl with the capers, olives, red peppers, lemon juice, remaining olive oil and some salt and pepper to taste. Toss all this together.

Put the potatoes on a large, flat serving plate. Scatter the salad on top and then arrange the *coppa* over this. Finally, place the chicken (with or without skewers) on top and drizzle with the truffle oil. Serve straight away, with lemon wedges and good, fresh bread.

SEAFOOD SALAD WITH COOKED LEMON AND CORIANDER JEMIMA BURRILL

SERVES 4

This version of a seafood salad is best served on top of thinly sliced raw fennel, or bruschetta rubbed with a little garlic and drizzled with olive oil (see page 54). Use any combination of scallops, prawns, squid or a firm, white fish – whatever looks best at the fishmonger's.

1 lemon
3 tablespoons olive oil
2 bay leaves
1 tablespoon fennel seeds
400g/14oz piece of halibut or similar cut
    into slices 2cm/³/₄-inch thick
8 small cleaned squid, cut into rings 2cm/
    ³/₄-inch thick, tentacles detached
4 large raw tiger prawns, peeled, de-veined
    and decapitated
8 fresh scallops
a handful of coriander leaves
salt and freshly ground black pepper

Put the lemon in a pan with water to cover and boil for half an hour or until soft. When it has cooled, cut it up into small pieces, discarding the pips, and place in a large serving bowl – be sure not to lose any of the zesty juice. Add the olive oil and some freshly ground black pepper.

Steam all the seafood, one sort at a time, either in a steamer or in a colander with a lid, set over a pan of boiling water. Add the bay and fennel seeds and a little salt to the water. First steam the halibut, which will take about 7 minutes; it's better to take it out a little underdone as it will continue to cook in its own heat. Add to the lemon in the serving bowl. Then steam the squid rings and tentacles for about 5 minutes or until they are tender and lose their translucency. Plunge them into cold water to stop the cooking and drain well. Add to the serving bowl.

Steam the prawns for about 5 minutes or until they have turned pink. Plunge into cold water, then drain and add to the serving bowl. Finally, slice the scallops in half horizontally, trying to keep the orange corals attached. Steam them as briefly as possible, just until they become opaque. Add them to the bowl and stir well. Add the coriander leaves, then taste and season with salt and add more olive oil if necessary.

SPANISH ROAST VEGETABLE SALAD

ESCALIVADA KATE LEWIS

SERVES 4–6

This dish isn't sure if it's a salad or a stew but it is lovely both as an accompaniment to meat or fish and as a dish on its own. If you can cook the vegetables on an open fire or barbecue, so much the better, as the flavour will be much improved. Otherwise, roast them in a hot oven.

2 large baking potatoes
3 aubergines
3 red peppers
2 red onions
extra virgin olive oil
10 basil leaves, torn
2 courgettes, cut into 2cm/³/₄-inch pieces
sea salt and freshly ground black pepper

Pierce the skin of each potato and aubergine 3 or 4 times with a fork or sharp knife. Place all the vegetables except the courgettes on a baking sheet and roast on the top shelf of an oven preheated to 220°C/gas mark 7, until they are cooked through and the skins are evenly coloured (or, alternatively roast them over a hot fire or barbecue). The peppers and aubergines will need 20–30 minutes and the potatoes and onions up to an hour.

When the vegetables are cool enough to handle, peel them and roughly break them into large chunks. Dress the aubergines and potatoes generously with olive oil, salt, pepper and some of the torn basil and mix together in a serving dish.

Season the courgettes and then fry them in olive oil until lightly coloured and tender. Lay them on top of the aubergine and potatoes with the peppers and onions. Season well, add the remaining basil and dress with more olive oil. Serve hot or at room temperature.

MEALS ON TOAST

ABOUT BRUSCHETTA

Bruschetta is nothing more than grilled bread, rubbed with garlic, then salted and drenched in olive oil. Yet it is incredible how this can be ruined. The bread should take the form of long slices cut from the centre of a day-old round Italian country loaf. These are normally sourdough. Don't attempt to make bruschetta from soft, bleached white bread. It must be grilled on a barbecue or, at a pinch, on a ridged chargrill pan; don't even think about using a toaster.

Rub the grilled bread with a peeled clove of garlic, then sprinkle with crunchy coarse sea salt or Maldon salt and drizzle with your best extra virgin olive oil. The oil is the whole point of bruschetta, so don't be thrifty with either the quality or the quantity. A really ripe tomato can be rubbed crudely on to the bread before the olive oil to make a Catalan *pa amb tomaquet*.

BRUSCHETTA WITH WARM RICOTTA SALAD DAVID EYRE

SERVES 4

Try to buy ricotta loose rather than in tubs, from a deli that has a good turnover, as it has a much better flavour when very fresh. Warming it is a good way of improving the flavour of bland commercial brands. If you can find authentic ewe's milk ricotta, then buy it straight away – ricotta should be the by-product of Pecorino cheese.

1 garlic clove, finely chopped
3 spring onions, finely chopped
finely chopped mint, basil and flat-leaf
  parsley, about 4 tablespoons in total
400g/14oz ricotta cheese
3 tablespoons olive oil
juice of 1 lemon
4 slices of bruschetta (see page 54)
a few fat black olives, pitted
a few fresh broad beans (optional)
freshly ground black pepper

Mix together the garlic, spring onions, herbs, ricotta, oil, lemon juice and black pepper and warm gently in a pan or low oven. Pile on to the bruschetta and scatter over some olives and, if in the season, some raw, shelled and peeled broad beans.

BRUSCHETTA WITH MOZZARELLA, TREVISO AND BALSAMIC VINEGAR

TOM NORRINGTON-DAVIES

SERVES 4

Treviso is a type of radicchio, or red chicory. It has a deep burgundy colour and, unlike the more common round *radicchio di Verona*, long, slender leaves. You could use round radicchio or white chicory for this recipe, but if you can hunt it out Treviso really is a find. It is very bitter, which is why I always bake it with a little sugar, but you can omit this if you prefer.

Another variation of this recipe, perhaps for a warm day, is to leave everything uncooked except for the bruschetta. The crunchy bitter leaves of the Treviso are a great foil for the silky, bland mozzarella.

2 heads of radicchio di Treviso
extra virgin olive oil
balsamic vinegar
1 teaspoon sugar
4 slices bruschetta (see page 54)
3 tablespoons roughly chopped fresh
  oregano or 1 tablespoon dried oregano
3 x 125g balls of mozzarella, each cut into
  4 slices
sea salt and freshly ground black pepper

Heat the oven to its highest setting. Cut the Treviso into quarters lengthways and place them on a baking tray. Drizzle with some olive oil and a little balsamic vinegar, then sprinkle the sugar over everything and season with a little salt and pepper. Cover with foil and bake for about 15 minutes, until the leaves have wilted and the heart has softened.

Lay 2 Treviso quarters on each bruschetta and then put 3 slices of mozzarella on top of that. Scatter the oregano over the whole thing and place the bruschetta in the tray in which you baked the Treviso. Hopefully there will be a little debris and juice left behind, which the bruschetta will mop up.

Bake briefly until the mozzarella has melted. This will only take a couple of minutes. Season with a little more balsamic vinegar and sea salt, then serve.

BRUSCHETTA WITH ROAST TOMATOES AND GRILLED SARDINES

DAVID EYRE

SERVES 4

Sardines on toast, my way, and just the thing for the garden on a hot day. To make a starter for an informal lunch, use any form of anchovies (see page 115) in place of sardines.

12 fresh sardines, scaled and gutted
16 roast tomatoes (see page 168)
4 slices of bruschetta (see page 54)
2 lemons
salt

Salt the sardines all over, especially the head and tail. Grill on a barbecue (or on a chargrill pan or under the grill) for 2–3 minutes per side (it is easier to roll sardines over their backs when trying to turn them). Press the tomatoes on to the bruschetta and then lay the sardines on top. Squeeze the lemon all over. Eat the sardines using the bruschetta as a sort of plate or trencher, and then eat the now sardine-flavoured bread.

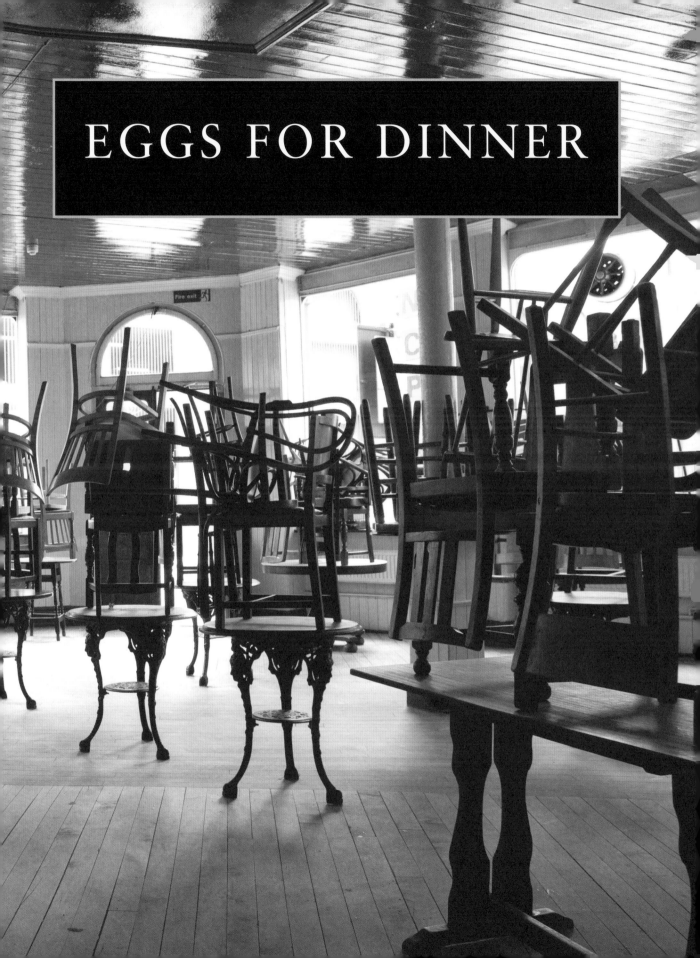

EGGS FOR DINNER

A NOTE ON EGGS

The days when the only eggs to be found on pub menus were of the questionable scotch variety (complete with day-glo breadcrumbs), are thankfully behind us. Not that there is anything wrong with a well-made scotch egg.

We take eggs for granted, but we shouldn't. A good egg is as richly flavoured as it is nourishing, with a creamy, amber yolk and a firm but not rubbery white. Some of this is down to careful cooking but the shopping is important, too. Happy hens lay better eggs. It's as simple as that. Try and buy your eggs from someone who can tell you where they came from and when they were laid. Small delis and farmers' markets are a better bet than a big store where the egg aisle stretches for half a mile. Try not to buy more eggs than you need: they shouldn't hang around for more than a week, ideally, and the best place for them is the larder, not the fridge.

Eggs can enrich the humblest of dishes, and, not surprisingly, feature strongly in the 'cucina rustica' of southern Europe, where meat was once scarce or expensive. The best example of such dishes might be the Spanish *Huevos a la Flamenca* (literally, gypsy eggs), on page 66, where the egg is a near-volcanic centrepiece to a stew of tomatoes and chorizo.

SMOKED HADDOCK WITH HORSERADISH MASH AND POACHED EGG TRISH HILFERTY

SERVES 6

One of the best light lunches ever. Buy undyed smoked haddock, which has a creamy colour (not yellow). The English smoked style is lighter in flavour than the Scottish, which is brined and then smoked over peat. The former uses larger fish; the latter is normally Finnan haddock, which are small split haddock.

6 x 200g/7oz pieces of smoked haddock
6 free-range eggs

For the court-bouillon
1.5 litres/2½ pints water
1 tablespoon white wine vinegar
bay, thyme and a few parsley stalks
6 black peppercorns
a pinch of salt

For the horseradish mash
1kg/2¼lb potatoes (such as Desirée, King Edward, Maris Piper or Spunta), peeled and halved
up to 300ml/½ pint milk (depending on the potato variety)
150g/5oz butter
2 tablespoons finely grated fresh horseradish
salt and freshly ground black pepper

Boil the potatoes until tender in just enough salted water to cover. Drain well, return to the pot and dry over a low heat until all the remaining moisture evaporates. Heat the milk, then add it to the pan and crush the potatoes with a potato masher. Beat in the butter, horseradish and a good grind of pepper. Adjust the seasoning and keep warm.

Meanwhile, make the court-bouillon. Put all the ingredients in a pan big enough to hold all the fish and bring to the boil. Turn down to a simmer and remove the herbs and peppercorns. Drop in the fish and cook gently until it is firm and no longer translucent. Give it a prod with a knife to check – it must be lightly cooked.

If you are feeling confident, poach the eggs alongside the fish. If not, do them in a separate pan.

Divide the mash and fish between 6 serving plates and put an egg on top of each portion. This tastes even better served with buttered sautéed spinach.

VARIATION
We often replace the horseradish mash with saffron mash – a very fine invention that appears all over the place but has to be attributed to (the guru) Simon Hopkinson, formerly of Bibendum restaurant. Infuse a gram of saffron in the milk (you may use a mixture of milk and cream) while it is heating through, and omit the horseradish. The in-joke here is that real smoked haddock and mash has white haddock and yellow mash instead of the other way round.

SALT COD TORILLA
TORTILLA DE BACALAO CARLOS VARGAS

SERVES 4–6

The name of this famous Spanish omelette comes from the word torta, or tart. The main difference between Spanish and French omelettes is that Spanish ones are flat whereas French ones are rolled. The former usually contain potatoes, too. Tortilla is eaten widely and often in Spain because of its versatility. It can be served hot or cold, in a sandwich or *bocadillo*, or as a quick *tapa*. There are countless variations on the basic tortilla but one of the tastiest ones is made with salt cod. You could also use roasted red peppers, chopped spinach or, for a spring vegetable tortilla, peas and broad beans.

300g/11oz salt cod, soaked (see page 122)
4 tablespoons olive oil
4 large potatoes, peeled and sliced
1 medium onion, sliced
8 eggs, beaten
a few sprigs of flat-leaf parsley, chopped
salt

Put the soaked salt cod in a large saucepan of simmering water and cook gently for 15–20 minutes, until the flesh is beginning to flake. Drain and leave to cool, discarding the skin and bones while it is still warm. Heat the oil in a large frying pan until smoking hot, add the potatoes and fry for a few minutes until golden. Then add the onion and cook for 3 minutes, covering the pan. The resulting condensation softens the potatoes and onion. Once the vegetables are cooked, take them out of the pan with a slotted spoon and mix with the beaten eggs and flaked salt cod. Add the parsley, and some salt if required.

Pour out about a tablespoon of the oil from the frying pan and tip in the tortilla mixture, cooking it over a very low heat until it is set underneath and coming away from the side of the pan. You may need to cover the pan to help cook the middle. To turn the tortilla, remove the pan from the heat, place a plate on it and turn the pan over so the tortilla is on the plate. Then slide the tortilla back into the pan and cook for 3 more minutes, uncovered.

GYPSY EGGS

HUEVOS A LA FLAMENCA DAVID EYRE

A robust down-home Andalucian supper dish.

100g/4oz Serrano ham, chopped
100g/4oz Spanish chorizo, chopped
olive oil
1 onion, finely chopped
2 garlic cloves, finely chopped
1 teaspoon paprika (preferably Spanish
   pimentón, which is smoked)
2 x 400g/14oz tins of chopped tomatoes
100g/4oz shelled peas or broad beans
10 new potatoes, sliced (leftovers are fine)
100ml/3½fl oz chicken stock or water
8 eggs
salt and freshly ground black pepper

Slowly cook the ham and chorizo in a little olive oil for 5 minutes. Remove the meat from the pan, add a little more oil, plus the onion, garlic and paprika and cook until the onion is soft. Add the tomatoes, peas or beans and potatoes with the chicken stock or water and some salt and pepper. Cover and cook for 10 minutes – or until the potatoes are done if you are using uncooked ones.

Divide the sauce between 4 individual ovenproof bowls, break 2 eggs into each and scatter the ham and chorizo over them. Then bake in a hot oven for 5–10 minutes, until the egg whites have set.

Afters

Pastel de Nata £1.20

Taleggio apple
& ras £6.50

Tapas

Smoked Pigeon breast
& mustard fruit £5.50

Olives £4
Roast tomato frittata £4

PASTA

COOKING DRIED PASTA

First of all, which dried pasta? Ignoring the artisan-made and sexily packaged Christmas gift type that costs silly money, there are some brands that are worth the extra. I am devoted to the De Cecco brand, but La Molisana is another favourite. Dried pasta is firmer and chewier than fresh or home-made pasta, which is, I think, its appeal.

When it comes to cooking it, lots and lots of boiling salted water is what's needed – around 5 litres/9 pints of furiously boiling water and at least 1 tablespoon of salt per 500g/1lb 2oz packet. Don't put oil in the water in the belief that it will stop the pasta sticking as it tends to 'wrap' the pasta while it swells, causing it to remain undercooked in the centre. By all means add oil to the water for fresh pasta (which only requires a couple of minutes to cook) but the only way to prevent gummy pasta is to cook it in lots of water and stir often. You also need a decent-sized colander to drain it in once it has reached *al dente*, but don't drain it too much – a little moisture helps the sauce join the pasta. After draining is the time to oil the pasta.

Cooking to the *al dente* stage means that it should give some resistance to the bite – the cooking times printed on the packets of De Cecco are precise. My per-person statistics are 75g/3oz for a starter and 100g/4oz for a main course.

BUCATINI WITH CAULIFLOWER, ANCHOVIES, PINENUTS AND RAISINS

JEMIMA BURRILL

SERVES 6

Use the wonderful, light green Romanesco cauliflowers (known as broccoli in Italy), if you can find them. A good variation is to add a pinch of saffron to the frying pan with the cauliflower.

2 heads cauliflower, cut into small florets (keep any leaves)
500g/1lb 2oz bucatini (or spaghetti)
5 tablespoons olive oil
1 large onion, thinly sliced
a pinch of dried chilli flakes
4 garlic cloves, finely chopped
75g/3oz pine nuts, toasted lightly in a dry frying pan
75g/3oz raisins, soaked in a little hot water for 15 minutes
50g/2oz tin of good-quality anchovies, drained and chopped
extra virgin olive oil
about 3 handfuls of flat-leaf parsley, roughly chopped
100g/4oz Parmesan cheese, freshly grated
salt and freshly ground black pepper

Boil the cauliflower florets in a large pan of salted water until not quite tender, then remove with a slotted spoon. Blanch any leaves in the same water, then remove. Add some more salt to the water and cook the pasta in it while making the sauce.

Heat the olive oil in a large frying pan, add the onion and chilli flakes and fry over a medium to high heat until the onion is tender and slightly browned. Add the cauliflower and continue cooking until it begins to soften but is still slightly crunchy. Now add the garlic, pine nuts and raisins. The garlic should brown a little but be careful not to let it burn. Reduce the heat to low, add the anchovies and stir until they disintegrate – about 5 minutes. Taste and season if necessary.

When the pasta is *al dente*, drain and add to the cauliflower mixture with a little water, adding enough extra virgin olive oil to coat the pasta thoroughly. Toss together with the parsley and half the Parmesan. Serve with the remaining Parmesan.

PENNE WITH SAUSAGE, TOMATO AND SAGE BRAD FOXWELL

SERVES 4

This recipe was brought to the Eagle by Paulo Santos. It was one of the first dishes I cooked here. I like it for its simplicity most of all, but also for its rough and ready-ness. It's very 'Eagle' – boisterous and filling.

3 tablespoons olive oil
6 good-quality pork and herb sausages
1 red onion, finely chopped
2 garlic cloves, finely chopped
400g/14oz tin of plum tomatoes, drained
400g/14oz penne pasta
10 sage leaves
4 tablespoons double cream
40g/1½oz Parmesan cheese, freshly grated
salt and freshly ground black pepper

Heat the oil in a frying pan. Peel the skins from the sausage and crumble the sausage meat into the oil, frying it gently until cooked. Add the onion and garlic and cook until soft and translucent. Then add the drained tomatoes and cook gently, covered, for 20 minutes or longer, until you have a thick sauce. Add the sage to the sauce 5 minutes before the end and season to taste.

Meanwhile, bring a large saucepan of salted water to the boil and cook the pasta until *al dente*. Drain and mix with the sauce. Add the cream and half the parmesan and mix well. Serve immediately, sprinkling the rest of the Parmesan over the top.

PENNE WITH ARTICHOKE HEARTS AND GREENS TOM NORRINGTON-DAVIES

SERVES 5

We like to use *cavolo nero*, or Italian black cabbage, at the Eagle for this pasta dish, because of its strong flavour and handsome colour. It is strictly a winter vegetable, not to be used before the first frosts, but other greens such as sprouting broccoli and kale make great substitutions in the spring.

For this dish to taste its best, you need the preserved artichokes sold in jars as antipasti. You will find them swimming in nasty polyunsaturated oil and this needs to be got rid of. It will be replaced by your own olive oil, of course, chock full of chilli and garlic.

2 or 3 garlic cloves
2 red chillies, seeded if you don't want too
*   much heat*
6 tablespoons extra virgin olive oil
500g/1lb 2oz penne pasta
2 or 3 heads cavolo nero (about 250g/9oz),
*   stripped from the thick stalk and finely*
*   sliced*
450g/1lb jar of artichoke hearts, drained and
*   roughly chopped*
100g/4oz Parmesan cheese, freshly grated
salt

Chop the garlic and chillies finely together. Stop chopping just short of ending up with a paste and combine them with the oil. Let this sit for about 10 minutes. That is enough time to put on a large pot of water for the pasta and prepare the cabbage and artichokes.

Add the pasta to the boiling water, then heat a large frying pan (or a wok) until it is smoking. Add the chilli oil and, very shortly afterwards, the cabbage. This will make a fierce popping sound. Fry for about 5 minutes, stirring all the time, then add the artichoke hearts. If the cabbage is frying too fiercely, add a tablespoon of water to the pan but don't reduce the heat. When the cabbage is tender and the contents of the pan are well and truly coated in the chilli oil, transfer to a large warmed bowl.

Drain the cooked pasta and quickly combine it with the sauce. Stir in the Parmesan just before serving. Season with salt and maybe a little more olive oil.

SPAGHETTINI WITH WALNUT SAUCE
TRISH HILFERTY

SERVES 6

A classic dish that requires the freshest of walnuts.

150g/5oz shelled walnuts
2 garlic cloves, crushed
20 sage leaves, chopped
135ml/4½fl oz olive oil
50g/2oz Parmesan cheese, freshly grated,
  plus extra to serve
2 tablespoons crème fraiche
500g/1lb 2oz Italian spaghettini
salt and freshly ground black pepper

Spread the walnuts out on a baking tray and roast them under a hot grill or in a moderate oven for a few mintues. Then skin them – this is best done by rubbing them vigorously in a tea towel while they are still hot, then tipping them into a colander and shaking until the skins fall to the bottom and out of the holes. Don't worry if you can't remove much of the skin.

Purée the garlic and sage with the olive oil in a food processor, then pulse in the nuts, keeping a rough texture. Fold in the Parmesan, crème fraiche and some pepper. Cook the spaghettini in a large pan of boiling salted water until *al dente*. Drain quickly and toss with the sauce, adding a little of the pasta cooking water.

ORECCHIETTE WITH BUTTER, SAGE, GARLIC AND PARMESAN DAVID EYRE

SERVES 4

This is exactly the thing to cook after you come home from work; the sauce takes the same time to make as the pasta takes to cook.
I think that you must use orecchiette – it is a chewy type of pasta that looks, as the name suggests, like little ears.

75g/3oz unsalted butter
450g/1lb orecchiette pasta
2 garlic cloves, crushed but left whole
20 or so sage leaves, finely chopped
4 tablespoons freshly grated Parmesan
  cheese

Clarify the butter by melting it over the lowest possible heat and then skimming off the bits that float on top. Gently pour the clarified butter into a clean pan, discarding the curds (or is it the wey?) that will have collected at the bottom. Meanwhile, cook the pasata in a large pan of boiling salted water until *al dente*, then drain.

Heat the butter with the garlic cloves and sage. When the garlic just begins to brown, remove it and throw it away. Mix the butter and sage with the orecchiette and Parmesan.

EGG FETTUCCINE WITH PORCINI, SAUSAGE AND PEAS

FETTUCCINE ALLA CIOCIANA FULVIA MARCONI

This is a strong winter dish which comes from my grandmother. She's from Ciociaria, a hilly area in the Lazio region of Italy, where the main ingredients (also my favourites) are commonly found.

20g/³/₄oz dried porcini mushrooms
1 tablespoon olive oil
¹/₂ small onion, finely sliced
1 small garlic clove, finely sliced
1 Italian fresh pork sausage, skinned and chopped
125g/4¹/₂oz peas
200g/7oz egg fettuccine
a knob of butter
2 tablespoons freshly grated Parmesan cheese
salt and freshly ground black pepper

Soak the porcini in 500ml/18fl oz warm water for 15 minutes, then drain, reserving the liquid. Heat the olive oil in a pan, add the onion and cook until lightly browned. Add the garlic and sausage and cook on a gentle heat for 5 minutes. Stir in the porcini and cook for 15 minutes. Now add the peas and stir in the water from the porcini bit by bit. Cover and cook for about 30 minutes, until the liquid has reduced to about half its volume. Season to taste.

Meanwhile, bring a large pan of water to the boil and cook the pasta until *al dente*. Drain, add the sauce, butter and Parmesan and mix together very well.

EGG FETTUCCINE WITH RICOTTA, PEAS AND SMOKED PANCETTA

DAVID EYRE

An elegant and lightweight pasta that uses half a dozen ingredients but relies on the quality of all of them. The peas must be young and fresh, the ricotta not very long ago milked from the sheep, and the bacon dry-cured, solid and sweet.

200g/7oz shelled young peas (about 500g/ 1lb2oz unshelled weight)
150g/5oz smoked pancetta or dry-cured smoked streaky bacon, cut into strips
50g/2oz butter
400g/14oz egg fettucine or tagliatelle
150g/5oz ricotta cheese
2 tablespoons freshly grated Parmesan cheese
a dozen basil leaves, torn as you use them

Boil the peas in salted water until just cooked, then drain. Gently melt the pancetta with the butter for 10 minutes or until the fat has run and the pancetta has become crisp. Add the peas to the pan and cook gently for a few minuets. Meanwhile, cook the pasta in a large pan of boiling salted water until *al dente*. Drain and mix in a warmed serving bowl with the ricotta, Parmesan and torn basil leaves. Reheat the peas and bacon and pour over the pasta.

SPAGHETTI WITH ROASTED FENNEL, LEMON AND CHILLI

TOM NORRINGTON-DAVIES

SERVES 2

I think that fennel bulbs are at their best in winter but this pasta dish is full of the promise of summer. It is very simple and addictive. If you are making it in warmer weather, replace the parsley with basil or oregano. Choose the fat female bulbs of fennel – they are much tastier than the flatter male bulbs.

1 fennel bulb
about 100ml/3¹/₂fl oz extra virgin olive oil
juice and ¹/₂ zest of 1 unwaxed lemon
¹/₂ red chilli, finely chopped
1 tablespoon capers, soaked in cold water
*   for 30 minutes, then squeezed and*
*   chopped*
1 garlic clove, finely chopped
200g/7oz spaghetti
75g/3oz Parmesan cheese
1 tablespoon chopped flat-leaf parsley
salt and freshly ground black pepper

Remove the little stalks and the tough outer layer from the fennel bulb. If there is a little of the herb (it looks like dill) poking out of the stalks, keep it and chop it up with the parsley. Cut the fennel in half down its length, then lay it cut-side down on a board and slice very finely, much as you would an onion.

Pour half the oil into a small roasting tray and add the fennel, lemon zest and half the juice, chilli, capers and garlic. Mix all the ingredients thoroughly with your hands. Season with salt and pepper and cover with foil. Place the tray on the top shelf of an oven heated to its highest setting and roast for about 20 minutes. Remove the foil and leave for another 10 minutes, until the fennel is slightly coloured and very tender.

This is now your pasta sauce; simply leave it to one side in a large bowl. In the time it takes to boil the spaghetti, it will not cool enough to need reheating. The pasta will do that for you. So cook the pasta until *al dente*, drain it and toss it around the bowl with the fennel mixture. Throw in two-thirds of the Parmesan and all the parsley, then check the seasoning. You may wish to use a little more of the oil and the remaining lemon juice.

Serve with the remaining Parmesan and some good bread for mopping up whatever's lurking at the bottom of the bowl when you've finished.

WHOLEWHEAT SPAGHETTI
WITH SARDINES DAVID EYRE

SERVES 4

An elemental dish from the Deep South of Italy that requires a handful of the freshest ingredients. Sardines, fennel, parsley and lemon are a terrific bright combo that makes a good foil to the earthy wholewheat pasta.

8 large fresh sardines
4 tablespoons extra virgin olive oil
2 garlic cloves, chopped
$^1/_2$ fennel bulb, finely chopped
400g/14oz wholewheat spaghetti
  (sometimes known as bigoli*)*
2–3 tablespoons chopped flat-leaf parsley
2 lemons
black pepper

To clean and fillet the sardines, gently rub the scales off each fish under a running tap, then run your thumb down its back to loosen the flesh from the spine. Cut off the head and slice open the belly down to the tail with a small, sharp knife. Pull out the innards and then open out the fish by running your thumb down one side of the spine. Lift the spine away, starting at the head, then break it off at the tail, so that you end up with a 'butterfly'. Wash the fillets, pat them dry and salt both sides lightly.

Heat half the oil in a pan large enough to fry 4 fillets at the same time. Fry half the garlic and fennel in the oil for 30 seconds or until the aroma rises. Slip 4 sardine fillets into the pan skin side down and then flip them over after a minute. Fry for another minute or so, until they are just cooked. Transfer the fillets to a plate and repeat with the remaining oil, garlic, fennel and sardines.

While the sardines are being fried, cook the pasta in a large pan of boiling salted water until *al dente*, then drain it and oil it a little. Add the parsley and pasta to the sardine pan and stir to coat with the flavoured oil. Lay the sardines on the pasta, season with black pepper and squeeze over the lemon juice.

PASTA & PESTO ALLA GENOVESE
TOM NORRINGTON-DAVIES

This is the classic way to present Genoa's famous (and much abused) basil sauce. If you are prone to buying pesto readymade, have a go at your own this time. It's a revelation.
If the thought of mixing pasta and potatoes doesn't grab you, try the pesto just as it is,

200g linguine
a large bunch of basil
50g pine nuts
2 garlic cloves, peeled
100ml extra virgin olive oil (a mild one is best)
3 heaped tablespoons freshly grated Parmesan cheese (or pecorino, if you prefer)
salt
2 medium-sized, waxy potatoes (approximately 400g)
100g dwarf beans (haricots verts)

Make the pesto first. Pesto should be a textured green sauce, not a super smooth emulsion. So, chop the basil, pine nuts and garlic roughly by hand and then crush them to a paste in a pestle and mortar. Alternatively, blitz them in a food processor, using the pulse button. Only then do you add the oil, not too fast, so that the sauce coheres. Finally, fold in the grated cheese, by hand. No more blitzing! Now you can season the pesto to taste with salt, adding more oil to loosen the sauce if it seems a bit stiff. Peel and dice the potatoes fairly finely. Boil them in plenty of salted water until tender but holding their shape. Set them aside. Top and tail the beans, then cut them into sections to roughly match the size of the potatoes. Blanch or steam them until just tender, then set them aside.

Finally, boil the pasta until it is done to your liking. Then drain it very briefly. Literally two shakes of the colander will do. You need a little dampness around the pasta to help it take the pesto. Return it to the pan, off the heat. Add 2 heaped tablespoons of the pesto, the potatoes and beans. Toss well. Serve with extra, freshly grated cheese, if you like.

BAKED BUCKWHEAT PASTA WITH SAGE, FONTINA AND CABBAGE PIZZOCCHERI

TOM NORRINGTON-DAVIES

SERVES 6

This baked pasta dish is a speciality of the Valetino. The name refers to both the type of pasta used – a buckwheat noodle roughly the shape of fettucine – and to this recipe, which as far as I know is pretty much the only way the noodle is served. I have had a hard time finding *pizzoccheri* in London. Some Italian delicatessens have it. If they don't you can get away with wholewheat spaghetti (my sincere apologies to any Milanese up in arms at the last remark).

This is quite a bulky meal – pasta, potatoes, cheese and cabbages! But it is very easy to prepare once you have exhausted yourself looking for the buckwheat pasta.

about 5 tablespoons extra virgin olive oil
a bunch of sage, finely chopped
2 garlic cloves, finely chopped
250g/9oz (usually one box) pizzoccheri
 pasta, broken up roughly into 5cm /2-inch
 pieces
1 Savoy cabbage, without the heart, roughly
 chopped (include as many of the dark
 outer leaves as you can; their flavour is a
 little more intense)
2 large waxy potatoes, peeled and diced
100g/4oz fontina *cheese, cut into small*
 cubes
100g/4oz unsalted butter, cut into small
 cubes
100g/4oz Parmesan cheese, freshly grated
salt and freshly ground black pepper

Gently heat about 3 tablespoons of the olive oil and infuse it with the sage and garlic over a very low heat for a few minutes. Be careful not to burn the sage.

Cook all the bulky ingredients – the pasta, cabbage and potatoes – separately in boiling water until just tender, then drain. Put them in a large mixing bowl and cover with the infused oil. Add the rest of the oil if you need it to stop the mixture sticking together. Mix together thoroughly and season with salt and pepper. Now transfer the mixture to a large shallow dish (a lasagne dish or gratin dish is ideal) and cover with the fontina and butter, followed by the Parmesan. Bake in an oven preheated to 180°C/gas mark 4 for about 30 minutes, until the mixture has warmed through and the Parmesan has browned slightly. Eat immediately, then lie down and sleep.

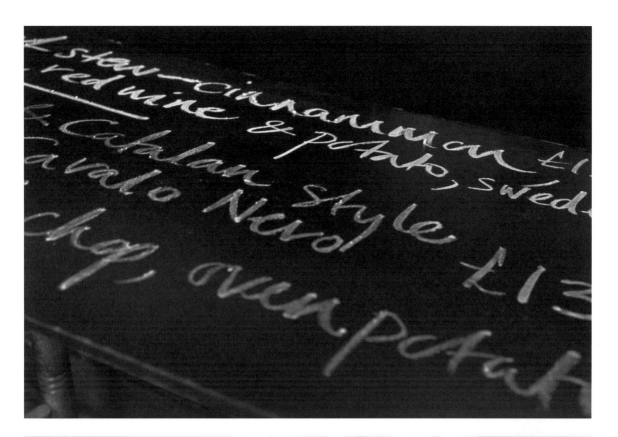

LASAGNE WITH RABBIT

TOM NORRINGTON-DAVIES

SERVES 6

Ask the butcher to chop the rabbits up for you, as it's a messy job. You want the legs, shoulders and the meaty part of the body (the saddle). Throw the rib cage away. Serve with a watercress salad, dressed simply with olive oil and lemon juice.

3 tablespoons olive oil
2 wild rabbits (about 2kg in total), jointed
   (see above)
3 garlic cloves, roughly chopped
2 onions, roughly chopped
a small bunch (about 30 leaves) of sage,
   roughly chopped
about 1/2 bottle of red wine
2 tablespoons tomato purée
1 teaspoon sugar
1 tablespoon butter
1 packet of lasagne pasta (how much you use
   will depend on the size of the baking dish)
salt and freshly ground black pepper

For the béchamel sauce
100g/4oz butter
50g/2oz plain flour
750ml/1 1/4 pints whole milk
a pinch grated nutmeg
100g/4oz Parmesan cheese, freshly grated

First, prepare the meat sauce. This can easily be done the day before you intend to eat this dish (indeed, all the better as the meat rests in the boozy gravy). If you do this, refrigerate as soon as it reaches room temperature.

Heat the olive oil in a large frying pan. Brown the rabbit pieces all over and then place to one side in a casserole. Lower the heat under the pan, add the garlic, onions and sage and fry until soft and translucent – don't worry if they catch a little. Pour in the wine and stir thoroughly so that it deglazes the pan a little. Add the tomato purée, sugar and some salt and pepper and pour all this

over the rabbit pieces. If it does not quite cover the rabbit, top it up with some boiling water from the kettle. Add the butter, then cover the casserole, place it over a high heat and bring to simmering point. Lower the heat and cook for about 1 1/2 hours or until the rabbit is very tender. It should be literally falling off the bone. If it begins to look a little short on juice while cooking, do add a bit more water. You will have plenty of opportunity to correct the seasoning later on. When the rabbit is cooked, leave it to cool and drain off all the gravy. Keep this to one side. Pick all the rabbit meat off the bones and put it back into the gravy, then check the seasoning.

To make the béchamel sauce, gently melt the butter in a small pan and stir in the flour. Let it eat up all the butter; at this point things will look pretty unpromising. Cook over a low heat for 3–4 minutes, then slowly add the milk, stirring continuously, and bring to the boil. When you have a creamy white sauce, about the consistency of single cream, remove from the heat and season with nutmeg, salt and pepper. Stir in two-thirds of the grated Parmesan.

Now you are ready to build the lasagne. Grease a baking dish well. Start with a layer of the rabbit mixture and top this with pasta. Top the pasta with a thin coating of the white sauce. Now start again with the rabbit, finishing with pasta and white sauce. Cover the top with the remaining Parmesan – this can all be done well ahead of the meal. Bake for approximately 35 minutes at 180°C/Gas mark 4. I always start a lasagne on a low shelf or covered with foil. This stops the Parmesan browning too fast. About 10 minutes before the cooking time is up, test the pasta for softness with a fork and transfer the dish to the top shelf until the cheese is as browned as you fancy it.

RICE

RISOTTO LAW

I used to be terrified of attempting to cook a risotto. I imagined that it was best left to Italian mothers, since it required years of practice, and anyway surely you had to have been brought up in the northern provinces of Italy. Perhaps I should just buy the finished dish from those who know, I thought. In reality, like many Italian dishes, it has a well-defined method that can be mastered if approached carefully and intelligently. Be aware, though, of the many sins that are committed in risotto's name: a rice dish that has not been made with specific Italian varieties of rice (which allow the soft starch to be released and dissolved into the liquid, thus creamily binding the grains with the other ingredients) will never be a risotto.

The basic method holds for all the styles – the Veneto style is looser, while in Piedmont and Lombardy risotto is more compact and substantial. The latter is often served with sausages, grilled pork, *osso bucco* (see page 104) and the like. Almost any vegetable combination can form the basis of a risotto – notwithstanding the more ridiculous frivolities of *la nuova cucina*. As ever, my favourite recipes are the simplest.

THE RISOTTO RULES

• Choose the superfino classified rice, i.e. with large, fat grains. Arborio is the most popular. It has a thin outer layer which releases its starch easily but leaves the grains nutty and separate. Carnaroli is prized for the perfect texture it provides. Vialone nano is a semifino variety and best for the Venetian loose style – terrific for Seafood Risotto (see page 98) and risotto made with young vegetables. In all cases allow about 50–60g/2–2$\frac{1}{4}$oz rice per person as a starter and 75g/3oz as a main course.

• You will need a heavy, thick-bottomed pan for cooking the risotto in. Stainless steel and enamelled cast iron are the best. Aluminium is not suitable, as the risotto will catch and cook unevenly.

• The stock must be light and well strained, so its flavour will not overpower the base ingredients. Make a chicken stock by putting some wings or drumsticks in a large saucepan with a leek, a carrot, an onion, a stick of celery, some bay leaves and some peppercorns. Cover with cold water and bring to a simmer – don't let it boil, even for a minute, or it will become cloudy with emulsified fat. Simmer for 45 minutes, then strain and return to the stove over a low heat – the stock must be hot when it is added to the risotto base. Substitute about 50g /2oz broken dried porcini mushrooms (known as *bricciollini*, and much cheaper than the sliced ones) for the chicken if making a vegetarian mushroom risotto. If making a seafood risotto, simply steam open the shellfish with a splash of white wine in a covered pan to release their juices, then dilute these with water to use as the cooking liquid.

• Start the risotto by frying the finely chopped vegetables in butter. Salt added at this stage will help the vegetables to release moisture and become transparent without browning. Follow with the rice and continue cooking for a few minutes until it is toasted or opaque and beginning to stick to the pan, but don't let anything brown.

• I often add some wine at this stage, let it reduce and then follow with the stock. Add the stock to the rice mixture in stages, adding only enough to be absorbed within a few minutes. Keep stirring the mixture gently and repeat the applications of stock perhaps up to 6 times. Cooking times will vary: you must judge it by taste, but 20 minutes is my estimate. The objective is for the rice to be tender and luscious but never too soft in the centre.

• The last stage is performed off the heat, when the risotto is judged to be nearly done, and is known as il mantecatura: melt a large knob of butter on the surface of the cooked risotto, with the lid on, and then beat in a good tablespoon of Parmesan. Don't use any cheese with seafood risotto – it is regarded, quite correctly, as very, very wrong.

A WORD ON PAELLA

Some Spanish and Portuguese dishes utilise a short-grained rice similar to the Italian varieties. Rice grown near Valencia in Spain is used for the famous Paella dishes of this region. Spanish 'Arroz' behaves slightly differently to Italian risotto, and produces less creamy results. Some of this is down to the cooking method. Whereas a risotto is always on the move around the pan, a Paella is barely stirred: this means that less of the starchy, outer layers in the rice are broken down. You can ape paella using Italian rice, but it won't be quite so nutty or pearly as the real thing. Luckily, many supermarkets and delis now carry 'paella rice'. Our favourite variety is Calasparra, often sold in handy 1-kilo sacks. It is worth seeking out one of these for the recipes on pages 100 and 103.

RISOTTO WITH BROAD BEANS AND MINT

TOM NORRINGTON-DAVIES

This is my favourite risotto. Although you can make risotto with frozen broad beans, this one relies on the starchiness of fresh beans. It is incredibly simple to make but there is one fiddly task ahead of cooking. After you have podded the broad beans they must be shucked – i.e. taken out of their little grey sacs. This not only makes them more digestible but also reveals their true colour, a stunning bright green. Here is how to make it easy. Drop the podded broad beans into a pan of boiling salted water and leave for about 30 seconds, then drain and cool them quickly under cold running water. Take a bean in one hand and aim it at a large bowl. Squeeze gently between your forefinger and thumb. The bean will pop out of the membrane and fall into the bowl in two neat halves. Remember that the skill is in a gentle squeeze. Don't be brutal or you will squash the bean and miss the bowl. It takes some time but don't cheat. You could use fresh, but not frozen, peas instead of broad beans and you could also substitute basil, marjoram or oregano for mint.

about 3kg/6½ lb fresh broad beans
    (400g/14oz podded and shucked weight –
    see above)
2 tablespoons extra virgin olive oil
    (optional)
about 2 litres/3½ pints vegetable or chicken
    stock
150g/5oz unsalted butter
2 onions, finely chopped
2 garlic cloves, finely chopped
300g/11oz arborio rice
a glass of white wine
a bunch of mint, chopped
about 75g/3oz Parmesan cheese, freshly grated
salt and freshly ground black pepper

The first thing I do for this recipe involves a food processor and is entirely optional. I put roughly half the broad beans in a food processor with the olive oil and pulse them roughly for about 20 seconds to make a loose paste. If the paste is too stiff, add a drop of water and pulse again very quickly. This adds a creamy base to the risotto and makes the colour a little more intense.

Put the stock in a pan and bring it to simmering point. Gently heat 100g/4oz of the butter in a separate pan, add the onions and garlic with a little salt and fry gently until tender. Do not let them brown. Turn the heat up high and pour in the rice. Stir it with a wooden spoon for about half a minute, coating it with the butter; do not let it stick to the pan. Add the wine and let it bubble fiercely for about a minute, stirring gently all the time. Quickly stir in the broad bean paste, if using, then reduce the heat and start to add the hot stock in stages as described on pages 92–93. When the rice is done, remove from the heat, add the rest of the butter and cover the pan until it has melted. Stir it in with the broad beans and mint, then add the Parmesan and some seasoning. Serve immediately.

RISOTTO WITH SAGE AND LEMON

TOM NORRINGTON-DAVIES

SERVES 5–6 AS A STARTER

Like the classic Milanese risotto (see page 100), this is incredibly simple to make, so it is worth being picky about the ingredients. Buy unsprayed, unwaxed lemons because you will be grating the rind from them. Good stock and well-aged *Parmiggiano Reggiano* (Parmesan) cheese are essential. The herb I love for this risotto is sage, but any of the woody herbs will do, rosemary or thyme in particular.

*about 2 litres/3$\frac{1}{2}$ pints vegetable or
    chicken stock*
2 tablespoons olive oil
100g/4oz unsalted butter
2 onions, finely chopped
2 garlic cloves, finely chopped
300g/11oz arborio rice
juice and grated rind of 2 lemons
a bunch of sage, finely chopped
1 teaspoon dried chilli flakes (optional)
*about 75g/3oz Parmesan cheese, freshly
    grated*
salt and freshly ground black pepper

Put the stock in a pan and bring it to simmering point. Heat the olive oil and 75g/3oz of the butter in a pan, add the onions and garlic with a little salt and fry gently until soft and translucent. Do not let them brown. Add the rice and turn the heat up high. Stir thoroughly for half a minute or so, until the rice is coated with the butter. Add the lemon juice and sage, plus the dried chilli if using. Turn the heat down and start adding the stock in stages, as described on pages 92–93. When the rice is done, remove from the heat, add the remaining butter and cover the pan until it has melted. Stir the butter in with the lemon rind and Parmesan, then season to taste and serve immediately.

SMOKED HADDOCK RISOTTO WITH SAFFRON, FENNEL AND PEAS

DAVID EYRE

A sort of arty kedgeree for six.

750g/1lb 10oz skinned, undyed smoked
   haddock
1 leek
1 carrot
2 fennel bulbs
1 small onion
a good bunch of parsley
a good bunch of coriander
175g/6oz butter
450g/1lb risotto rice (arborio is fine)
1g (a decent pinch) of saffron threads
175g/6oz peas (frozen petits pois will do)
100ml/3½fl oz white wine
a squeeze of lemon juice
salt and freshly ground black pepper

For the court-bouillon
1 small onion, chopped
1 carrot, chopped
1 bay leaf
a few parsley stalks
3 litres/5 pints water
a splash of white wine

To make the court-bouillon, put all the ingredients in a large pan and bring to a gentle simmer. Add the smoked haddock and poach until just cooked, then remove the fish, flake it and set aside. Strain the poaching liquid and dilute it sufficiently to achieve a lightly flavoured stock – keep hot.

Finely chop the leek, carrot, fennel, onion, parsley and coriander – in a food processor if you have one. Soften this mixture in 100g/4oz of the butter with a pinch of salt in a heavy pan. Add the risotto rice and cook for a couple of minutes at a moderate rate until most of the rice has turned opaque. Add the saffron threads, peas and white wine. After a minute, add enough hot stock just to cover the rice mixture and stir gently until most of it has been absorbed. Continue adding the stock in stages, as described on pages 92–93, until the rice is done. The grains should have fluffed up and the mixture become creamy. Stir in the smoked haddock, remove from the heat, then add the remaining butter and cover the pan. When the butter has melted, stir it in with a squeeze of lemon, check the seasoning and serve.

SEAFOOD RISOTTO

DAVID EYRE

SERVES 6

This is a truly classic risotto from the Veneto, and fortunately all the seafood is easily available outside Italy. Use any combination of mussels, clams, scallops, prawns, small squid or cuttlefish.

about 500g/1lb 2oz mussels
about 500g/1lb 2oz clams
a glass of white wine
1 onion, finely chopped
1 carrot, finely chopped
1 fennel bulb, finely chopped
1 celery stick, finely chopped
2 garlic cloves, finely chopped
75ml/2½fl oz olive oil
175g/6oz unsalted butter
200g/7oz cleaned small squid, cut into strips
200g/7oz raw prawns, shelled
450g/1lb risotto rice, preferable vialone nano
about 4 tablespoons chopped flat-leaf parsley
200g/7oz cleaned fresh scallops, cut in half if they are king scallops
juice of 1 lemon
salt and freshly ground black pepper

Scrub the mussels and clams, discarding any open ones that don't close when tapped, then purge them of grit by soaking them in several changes of cold water. Put the mussels in a large saucepan with the white wine, cover and leave over a high heat for a few minutes, until just opened. Remove them from the pan with a slotted spoon and set aside, then add the clams to the pan and cook them in the same way. Remove them from the pan and dilute the cooking liquid with 2 litres/3½ pints of water. Strain this stock and keep it hot in a pan over a low heat.

In a heavy pan, fry the vegetables and garlic in the olive oil and 100g/4oz of the butter with black pepper and a little salt for a couple of minutes. Add the squid and prawns and continue cooking for a few more minutes. Add the rice and fry until it becomes opaque. Stir in the chopped parsley, then add the scallops, mussels and clams. Add the stock in stages as described on pages 92–93. Aim for a fairly loose, almost runny risotto. Remove from the heat, add the remaining butter and cover the pan. When it has melted, stir it in with the lemon juice and serve.

RISOTTO NERO
HARRY LESTER

Inspired by the Trattoria Alla Madonna which is a stone's throw from the Rialto Bridge in Venice, this classic risotto brings a little taste of Italy to the Farringdon Road. The stew is also rather good served on polenta or with spaghetti.

For the gremolata topping and the cuttlefish stew

1 lemon
1 bunch of fresh parsley, stalks and leaves separated and each finely chopped
4 garlic cloves, finely chopped
2 tablespoons olive oil
1 red chilli, finely chopped (de-seed if you don't want the heat)
2kg/4^1/$_2$lb cuttlefish (ask your fishmonger to clean the fish, reserving the ink sacs), cut into 2–3cm pieces
1 tablespoon tomato purée
1 bay leaf
175ml/6fl oz dry white wine

For the risotto

100g/3^3/$_4$oz butter
1 tablespoon mild olive oil
1 onion, finely chopped
1 stick of celery, finely chopped
1.5 litres/2^1/$_2$ pints fish, vegetable or very light chicken stock (preferably homemade)
500g/1^1/$_4$lb carnaroli or arborio rice
175ml/6fl oz dry vermouth
175ml/6fl oz dry white wine
salt and freshly ground black pepper

First make the gremolata topping. Combine the zest of the lemon, the chopped parsley leaves and 2 cloves of the finely chopped garlic. Set aside.

Next, make the cuttlefish stew. In a large heavy-based pan warm the olive oil over a moderate heat. Add the parsley stalks, chilli and remaining garlic. Just as they begin to show signs of colouring, add the cuttlefish. Turn the heat up and stir to coat. Cut the zested lemon in half. Add the tomato purée, half the lemon, the bay leaf, white wine and the reserved cuttlefish ink, season with salt and pepper and cover tightly. Reduce the heat to the lowest setting, cover tightly and cook, stirring occasionally, for an hour or until tender.

Now make the risotto. In a large heavy-based pan melt half of the butter and the oil over a moderate heat. Add the chopped onion and celery and season with salt. Cook the vegetables gently until soft but still light in colour. Add the cuttlefish stew to the pan and warm through. Pour the stock into a separate pan and heat it until piping hot.

Add the rice to the pan with the vegetables and cuttlefish and stir it thoroughly using a wooden spoon (a metal one can break the rice). When the rice is completely coated in the oil and butter mixture, add the vermouth and white wine and stir continually, until absorbed. Gradually add the hot stock, a ladleful at a time, stirring constantly until all the liquid is absorbed and the rice is tender.

To serve, dice the remaining butter and stir it into the risotto. Squeeze the juice of the remaining half of the zested lemon over everything and top with the gremolata. Italians never add cheese to fish risottos.

OSSO BUCO, RISOTTO MILANESE & GREMOLATA JAKE HODGES

SERVES 4

Osso bucco (which means 'bone with a hole') is one of those luxurious down-home dishes that any cook loves to make. It is sometimes cooked *in bianco* – without tomatoes – but I prefer this version, with the tomatoes liaising the vegetables and vermouth. Ask for the osso bucco to be cut for you and pay extra to have the centre cuts of each shin. The Milanese style is to serve the meat with a plain saffron risotto and gremolata – a mixture of finely chopped lemon rind, garlic and parsley – as a seasoning.

50g/2oz butter
3 tablespoons olive oil
4–8 pieces (depending on their diameter) of veal shin (osso bucco), cut 4cm/1^1/$_2$-inches thick
50g/2oz plain flour, seasoned with salt and pepper
2 carrots, finely chopped
1 onion, finely chopped
2 celery sticks, finely chopped
4 garlic cloves, finely chopped
175ml/6fl oz dry vermouth
400g/14oz tin of Italian plum tomatoes, chopped
salt and freshly ground black pepper

For the gremolata
2 teaspoons finely grated lemon rind
1 garlic clove, very finely chopped
2 tablespoons finely chopped parsley
1 tablespoon olive oil
a pinch of salt

For the risotto
2 litres/3^1/$_2$ pints chicken stock
a pinch saffron
150g/5oz butter
2 tablespoons olive oil
1 red onion, finely chopped
1 celery stick, finely chopped
250g/9oz arborio rice
4 tablespoons dry vermouth or white wine
4 tablespoons freshly grated Parmesan cheese

Heat the butter and oil in a large, heavy-based casserole with a tight fitting lid. Dust the osso bucco in the seasoned flour and then brown it carefully in the hot fat. Remove the meat and add a little more fat to the pan if needed. Add the carrots, onion, celery and garlic and turn the heat down, then cook, stirring occasionally, for 10 minutes. (If the vegetables start to stick to the pan, add a little of the vermouth, which should loosen them.) When the vegetables have softened, turn the heat up and add the tomatoes. Boil vigorously for 2–3 minutes to drive off some of the liquid and intensify the flavour. Then add the rest of the vermouth and carry on the fierce cooking for another few minutes to drive off the alcohol. Check the seasoning. Place the osso bucco back in the pan, cover with a circle of wet greaseproof paper and put the lid on tightly. Turn the heat down to its lowest setting and cook for 2 hours or until the meat is completely tender. Alternatively, this last part of the cooking can be done in an oven preheated to 150°C/gas mark 2.

Mix together all the ingredients for the gremolata and set aside.

To make the risotto, put the stock in a pan and bring to boiling point. Put the saffron in a cup, pour over some of the stock and set aside. Melt 75g/3oz of the butter with the oil in a heavy-based pan, add the onion and celery and cook gently with a little salt for about 15 minutes, until tender. Add the rice, turn the heat up and stir to coat the rice with the fat. After a couple of minutes, add the vermouth or wine and let the alcohol evaporate for a moment or two. Then stir in a couple of cups of the hot stock and the saffron stock. Add the remaining stock in stages, as described on pages 92–93, until the rice is done.

Remove from the heat, put the remaining butter on top and cover with a lid. When the butter has melted, stir it in with the Parmesan.

Serve the risotto immediately, topped with the osso bucco. Either sprinkle the gremolata on top or pass it round for everyone to help themselves.

PAELLA VALENCIANA

CARLOS VARGAS

SERVES 4–6

Paella originated in Valencia and its name derives from *paellera*, the wide, shallow, two-handled pan in which it is cooked. Contrary to what most people think, it was originally made with meat but these days shellfish is more popular. There are so many different theories about the right way to make paella that it's difficult to know which, if any, to accept. I will explain the main points here and leave the rest to your own interpretation.

Traditionally, *calasparra* rice is used. This is difficult to find unless you know of a Spanish shop, but it is similar to the Italian *arborio* rice, which is stocked by most supermarkets. Like arborio, calasparra is a round-grain rice which takes longer to cook than long-grain rice such as basmati. It absorbs liquid very slowly and then when the grains have swelled they release their starch all at once. Unlike a risotto, all the liquid is added to a paella in one go rather than in stages. You need a large flame, so if you don't have a big burner on your cooker it is probably best done on a barbecue.

2 ñoras *(Spanish sweet dried peppers, also known as* romescos*) or 1 red pepper, chopped*
150ml/¼ *pint olive oil*
500g/1lb 2oz *boneless chicken, cut into small pieces*
100g/4oz *boneless pork (leg or loin), cut into small pieces*
1 *small onion, finely chopped*
1 *small carrot, finely chopped*
2 *green peppers, chopped*
150g/5oz *fresh butter beans (or use drained and rinsed tinned ones)*
50g/2oz *peas*
4 *garlic cloves, finely chopped*
3 or 4 *tomatoes, skinned and finely chopped*

100g/4oz *live snails (or use scrubbed cockles or clams if you can't get live, purged snails)*
100g/4oz *cooked ham, diced*
500g/1lb 2oz calasparra *or arborio* rice
2 *tablespoons paprika*
1 *pinch of saffron strands*
1 *litre/1³/₄ pints hot chicken stock*
juice of 1 lemon
salt
lemon wedges, to serve

If using *ñoras*, soak them in hot water for an hour, then drain and tear them into pieces.

Heat the olive oil in a paellera at least 40cm/16 inches in diameter. Add the chicken and pork and fry until browned all over, then remove from the pan with a slotted spoon. Stir in the onion, carrot, green peppers, butter beans, peas, garlic and *ñoras* and cook until softened. Then add the tomatoes and wait until the juice runs, stirring several times. Add the snails (or cockles or clams) and ham. The heat will make the snails come out of their shells; at that moment add the rice. Stir well, return the chicken and pork to the pan and add the paprika and about 2 teaspoons of salt. Fry the mixture for 2 or 3 minutes so that the rice starts to catch, then add the saffron to the hot stock and pour it into the pan. When the paella starts to boil, add the lemon juice and turn the heat to low (the lemon juice prevents the rice becoming too sticky). It's best not to stir the paella now. Instead, move the pan occasionally so the heat is evenly distributed. When the rice is cooked (after about 15 minutes), cover with foil and leave to rest for 5 minutes. Adjust the seasoning if necessary and then serve with lemon wedges.

SPANISH RICE WITH RABBIT
ARROZ CON CONEJO CARLOS VARGAS

SERVES 6

This dish is juicier than paella because it is cooked in a deeper pot, a *cazuela*, allowing less water to evaporate during cooking. It's a very useful dish because it can be made with a wide variety of vegetables and a bit of leftover chorizo. The main ingredients, apart from the rabbit, are broad beans and peas. If possible, ask your butcher to chop up the rabbit for you. You need the legs, shoulders and the meaty part of the body (the saddle). Throw away the rib cage or use it to make the stock.

150ml/¼ pint olive oil
1.5kg/3¼lb rabbit, jointed
1 onion, chopped
5 garlic cloves, chopped
1 red and 1 green pepper, sliced
2 large tomatoes, chopped
2 carrots, finely chopped
2 sprigs of thyme
2 cured chorizos, sliced
500g/1lb 2oz calasparra *or* arborio *rice*
1 bay leaf
150g/5oz broad beans (podded weight)
100g/4oz peas (podded weight)
1 litre/1¾ pints hot rabbit, chicken or
   vegetable stock
1 tablespoon hot paprika
2 lemons
a handful of flat-leaf parsley, chopped
salt and freshly ground black pepper

Heat the olive oil in a casserole dish and fry the rabbit until it is browned on all sides. Add the onion, garlic, peppers, tomatoes, carrots and thyme and fry for 10 minutes over a medium heat. Then add the chorizo and fry until it releases its fatty juice.
Add the rice and stir well so that it absorbs the fat. Now add the bay, beans and peas. After 2 minutes, stir in the hot stock and the paprika. When the mixture starts to boil, reduce the heat and simmer for about 15 minutes or until the rice is almost cooked. Then take the pot off the heat and leave to rest for 10 minutes. Squeeze on the lemon juice, then season to taste, sprinkle with the parsley and serve.

FISH

PARTNERING FISH

Sweet, aromatic herbs such as flat-leaf parsley, coriander, tarragon, dill, chervil, oregano and basil can be used either in marinades for fish or in chopped raw salsas – see *salmoriglio*, opposite, for example. Herbs, chopped tomatoes, black olives and capers, mixed with lemon juice and olive oil, then warmed gently to make a dressing, make a good foil for simple grilled or baked fish. Lemon is essential for all fish. Gremolata, a barely-oiled chopped garnish of flat-leaf parsley, garlic, lemon rind and lemon juice (see page 100), is particularly good with simply cooked seafood.

The Provençal tapenade (see page 134) and *aioli* (a type of garlic mayonnaise) are very successful with cod and hake. Try very thinly sliced fennel embellished with parsley leaves, lemon and olive oil for oily fish such as tuna, swordfish and mackerel. Or thinly sliced, partially peeled and seeded cucumber, salted to purge it of excess moisture, then washed and dried and dressed with sherry vinegar and coriander leaves.

Other possibilities include roast or grilled fennel and tomatoes; spinach or young Swiss Chard sautéed with lemon or black olives and garlic; roast pepper salads using anchovies, basil and capers with grilled fish; quickly fried chanterelles or field mushrooms with garlic for firm white fish such as turbot, brill or halibut; mashed potatoes with baked cod or hake. And some people say they don't like fish?

ABOUT GRILLED FISH

Round, firm fish, such as sea bass, grey or red mullet, bream and sardines, are fantastic for grilling and, as with all fish, are tastier if cooked on the bone. This means a little more work for the eater but it is well worth it. As far as quantities go, 200g/7oz cleaned and gutted per person is a fair rule of thumb.

Heat a griddle pan or overhead grill. If you are using a whole fish, make 2 or 3 slashes to the bone on each side. If using a fillet, score or slash the skin to stop it curling up, but don't cut through the flesh. Lightly oil and season with sea salt and a good grinding of pepper. Fillets should be grilled for 2–4 minutes per side, depending on thickness, until the flesh is firm to the touch and just beginning to flake. Whole fish will take longer and if they weigh over 200g they should be cooked on a medium heat. They are done when the flesh is firm and just beginning to come away from the bone.

GRILLED TUNA WITH SALMORIGLIO AND NEW POTATOES JAKE HODGES

SERVES 4

Salmoriglio is a Southern Italian herb sauce that goes well with grilled fish and meat. It is strongly flavoured and should be treated with respect. Use the best olive oil you can afford. I have made it with oregano here but you can also make a very flavourful thyme *salmoriglio* as long as you use young, green thyme that will crush to a paste easily.

When buying the tuna, make sure you get fresh, not frozen, loin and ask the fishmonger to slice if for you rather than buying it ready sliced. Check that the fish doesn't look old and tired or grey but has a shiny complexion. It can be quite dark or pale, depending on which part of the loin and what type of tuna it is.

675g/1¹/₂lb new potatoes such as Jersey
  Royals, or waxy potatoes such as Pink Fir
  Apple or La Ratte, scrubbed clean
a sprig of mint (optional)
red wine vinegar, olive oil and chopped
  herbs for dressing the potatoes (optional)
4 x 150g/5oz fresh tuna steaks, about
  1.5cm/²/₃ inch thick
salt and freshly ground black pepper

For the salmoriglio
¹/₂ cup clean, well-dried oregano leaves
1 heaped teaspoon Maldon sea salt
2 tablespoons lemon juice
6–8 tablespoons good olive oil

First make the salmoriglio: put the oregano leaves and salt in a pestle and mortar and crush to a smooth paste. Mix in the lemon juice and then gradually add enough olive oil to make an emulsion.

Put the potatoes in a pan of cold water with some salt and the mint, if using, and bring to the boil. Simmer until tender, then drain well. If you like, you could toss the cooked potatoes with a few shakes of some very fine red wine vinegar and then with a little olive oil and whatever chopped herbs you fancy. I would probably use flat-leaf parsley and maybe a little mint, but there is no reason why you shouldn't use coriander, rocket or whatever else you have available.

To grill the tuna you need either a barbecue, in good weather, or a ridged grill pan or heavy-based frying pan. Whatever you use, it should be extremely hot before you add the fish. Season the tuna, going easy on the salt as the sauce will be quite salty, and then sear for about 45 seconds on each side, so it is medium rare. If it is cooked all the way through it will become dry and take on a rather different taste. If you don't like undercooked tuna, eat another fish.

Put the tuna on serving plates and spoon over the sauce, then serve with the potatoes.

GRILLED SQUID PIRI-PIRI

DAVID EYRE

SERVES 6

Piri-piri is a fierce Portuguese marinade and basting sauce, made originally from the small hot chillies of the same name, grown in Portugal's former African colonies. Grilled chicken is the more usual vehicle for piri-piri, but squid is the thing; though I would also recommend fresh tiger prawns and, if the occasion should arise, roast suckling pig. The squid should really be barbecued rather than grilled conventionally.

2 red peppers
2kg/4$\frac{1}{2}$lb fresh, not frozen, squid – this will
    provide just over 1kg/2$\frac{1}{4}$lb cleaned squid
    (see below)
6 fresh red chillies (or more), seeded
2 garlic cloves, chopped
3 bay leaves
2 teaspoons ground coriander
200ml/7fl oz olive oil
2 teaspoons sea salt
3 tablespoons wine vinegar

Grill the red peppers all over until the skin has blackened, then leave until cool enough to handle. Peel and seed them, then set aside.

Clean the squid. They are easier to clean than they look. Pull the head and tentacles away from the body, bringing the innards with them. Remove the plastic-like quill from inside the body, then wash the body – cut it open along its length to facilitate cleaning if necessary. Cut the tentacles off the head in one piece, just in front of the eyes, and trim the longer tentacles. Discard the head. Remove the 'beak' from the centre of the tentacles and discard it.

To make the marinade, purée the red peppers, chillies, garlic, bay and coriander in a blender or food processor. Stir in enough of the oil to make a loose paste. Marinate the squid in half of this paste for at least 4 hours. Mix the remaining paste with the salt, remaining oil and the vinegar to make the basting sauce, then taste to check that it is hot enough.

Grill the squid on a steady fire, basting it every minute or two (use a new paintbrush with natural bristles). Serve with a tomato salad and rice.

CHARMOULA MACKEREL

SAM & SAM CLARK

SERVES 4

Charmoula is a classic Moroccan spice mix which is widely used to flavour meat, fish and vegetables. Here it works well to counteract the rich flavour of the mackerel. Ask your fishmonger to prepare the mackerel fillets and then you simply have to marinate and cook it.

4 mackerel, cleaned and filleted

For the charmoula
2 garlic cloves
2 teaspoons cumin seeds, freshly ground
juice of 1 lemon
1/2 tablespoon red wine vinegar
3/4 teaspoon sweet paprika (preferably
 Moroccan)
8 tablespoons roughly chopped fresh
 coriander
2 tablespoons extra virgin olive oil
1 tablespoon olive oil (optional, for pan
 frying the fish)
black pepper
lemon wedges, to garnish
seasonal vegetables or salad, to serve

Using a pestle and mortar, pound the garlic with 1 level teaspoon of salt until a smooth paste is formed, then add the cumin followed by the lemon juice, vinegar, paprika, coriander, olive oil and pepper.

Place the mackerel on a baking tray and slash them half a dozen times on each side. Rub two-thirds of the charmoula mixture all over the fish. The remaining third can be kept in the fridge for up to a week. Cover the fish with cling film and allow it to marinate in the fridge for between 20 minutes and 2 hours.

The mackerel can be roasted, pan fried or grilled. To roast the mackerel preheat the oven to 220°C/gas mark 7 and cook it for 8 minutes. To pan-fry the fish, heat 1 tablespoon of olive oil in a large non-stick frying pan and cook the fish over a medium heat for 3–4 minutes on each side. To grill the mackerel, preheat the grill to medium and cook it for 3–4 minutes on each side. Serve the cooked fish immediately, with seasonal vegetables or salad and lemon wedges.

FRIED FILLETS OF FRESH ANCHOVIES

DAVID EYRE

SERVES 4

I've seen fresh anchovies recently in a couple of good London fishmonger's and they are generally available in the fish market, so your fishmonger should be able to get hold of them for you. If you have no joy wih your tame 'monger, then use very fresh sardines and follow the instructions for filleting them on page 83. Filleting anchovies is not as ridiculous a pastime as you might imagine, I promise; they can be done in under 30 seconds. Fresh anchovies can grow up to 20cm /8 inches in length but are normally around 10cm/4 inches long – much larger than one would think – and since they are delicate, no knife is required.

16 firm fresh anchovies
1 egg, beaten
2 tablespoons white wine
2 tablespoons finely chopped fresh flat-leaf
    parsley
4 tablespoons plain flour, seasoned with salt
    and pepper
2 tablespoons polenta or cornmeal
vegetable oil for frying
2 lemons
salt and freshly ground black pepper

Wash the anchovies in a bowl of water, then fillet them: hold a fish in one hand and run the edge of your thumb gently from the body cavity along one side of the spine towards the tail. Do this a couple of times until the fillet starts to fall away from the spine. Repeat on the other side and then, pinching the head, lift the spine from the fillets and break it off just in front of the tail. You should now have a 'butterfly', or double fillet.

Mix the beaten egg, wine and chopped parsley together in one bowl and the seasoned flour and polenta in another. Pour 3cm/ 1$\frac{1}{4}$ inches of vegetable oil into a wide pan and heat until hot but not smoking. Holding two opened fish together by the tail in a sort of fan arrangement, dip first in the egg and then in the flour and fry immediately. Adjust the heat so that they take around 2 minutes to brown. Drain and eat promptly with a squeeze of lemon. Repeat with the remaining fish.

ABOUT ANCHOVIES

Anchovies come in four forms:

Fresh: When they are filleted, floured and fried, these are the definitive fried fish. If, after frying, you marinate them in garlic-infused olive oil, vinegar, coriander and pepper, they can be served as a salad or tapa of anchovies *en escabeche*.

Marinated or soused in vinegar and oil: These are marinated raw, as in Spanish *boquerones* or the Italian *alici*. Don't use them for cooking but they are great with herbs or tomatoes on grilled bread (see page 54).

Salted and packed whole: My preferred form of larder anchovy. The flavour is unique, without any of the rank pungency many people associate with anchovies. They need to be desalted and filleted before use, which is easily done. Soak the fish in cold water for half an hour or so, then carefully rub them between your fingers to remove the skin – this divests them of overt saltiness. Use your thumb to remove the fillets, discarding the tail and tiny dorsal fin. If you don't intend to use the fillets immediately, pat them dry, layer them in a dish and cover with olive oil. They will keep like this in the fridge for a week but the flavour will diminish.

Cured tinned fillets in oil: Bear in mind that the best tinned anchovies are always going to be a little expensive, as they will have been filleted and packed by hand. They should be fat and pink, without hairy little bones, taste somewhat sweet and not at all over-salty.

When you are cooking salted or cured anchovies for, say, pasta, their flavour will more easily merge with other ingredients if they are chopped finely and then dissolved in oil. Do this double-boiler fashion – i.e. stir them into the olive oil in a small pot set within a large one of simmering water, until creamy. Never fry chopped anchovies in oil. They will quickly harden and become bitter.

FRIED MARINATED MONKFISH
RAPE EN ADOBO CARLOS VARGAS

This is an old gypsy recipe from the coast near Cadiz. Adobo is a kind of marinade that will preserve the fish for a few days, simultaneously giving it a wonderful flavour. A very easy recipe, it would also be suitable for hake, shark, cod or mackerel. It can be eaten as a light tapa dish or as a main course with rice, fried potatoes, tomato salad or sautéed spinach with garlic and lemon.

600g/1lb 5oz monkfish tail, skinned, boned
   and cut into large chunks
2 tablespoons plain flour
200ml/7fl oz olive oil
a squeeze lemon
lemon wedges, to serve

For the adobo
2 tablespoons olive oil
1 large onion, chopped
1 carrot, finely chopped
4 garlic cloves, chopped
a little bay, thyme and parsley
2 slices lemon
1 tablespoon paprika
1 tablespoon vinegar
salt

To make the adobo, heat the oil in a frying pan and fry the onion, carrot and garlic in it for 3 minutes. Add the bay, thyme, parsley, lemon slices, paprika, vinegar and some salt, then turn down the heat and cook gently for 8 minutes. Leave to cool.

Toss the monkfish with the adobo and leave for 2–3 hours in a cool place – the longer you leave it, the stronger the flavour will be.

Remove the fish from the adobo and toss it with the flour. Fry in the olive oil over a medium heat for about 4 minutes. Squeeze on a little lemon juice and serve immediately, with lemon wedges.

BAKED SEA BASS WITH TOMATOES

DAVID EYRE

SERVES 4

This is the easiest and most forgiving way to cook fish at home. Since the heat is less direct than with other methods, it may take a little longer than, say, grilling, but the trade-off is that timing is less critical and all you need is a shallow ovenproof dish or steel frying pan by way of equipment. Run the oven up to maximum heat, then reduce it to 200°C/gas mark 6 when putting the fish in.

You'll need a single fish weighing around 800g/1lb 12oz (or 2 smaller ones) scaled, gutted and trimmed of its fins. Slash the fish two or three times on each side so that it will cook evenly, season it well inside and out and put it in an ovenproof dish. Slice 8 large, properly ripe tomatoes and lay them around the fish. Scatter sliced, not chopped, garlic, basil leaves and a couple of chopped anchovies over the tomatoes. Lubricate with olive oil and a little white wine. Bake at 200°C/gas mark 6 for around 25 minutes, or until the fish is firm to the touch and the flesh just starts to flake when prodded with a knife. Leave the fish to rest for a few minutes, then serve with something as uncomplicated as plain rice or bread, or nothing at all.

Sea bream is every bit as perfect cooked this way.

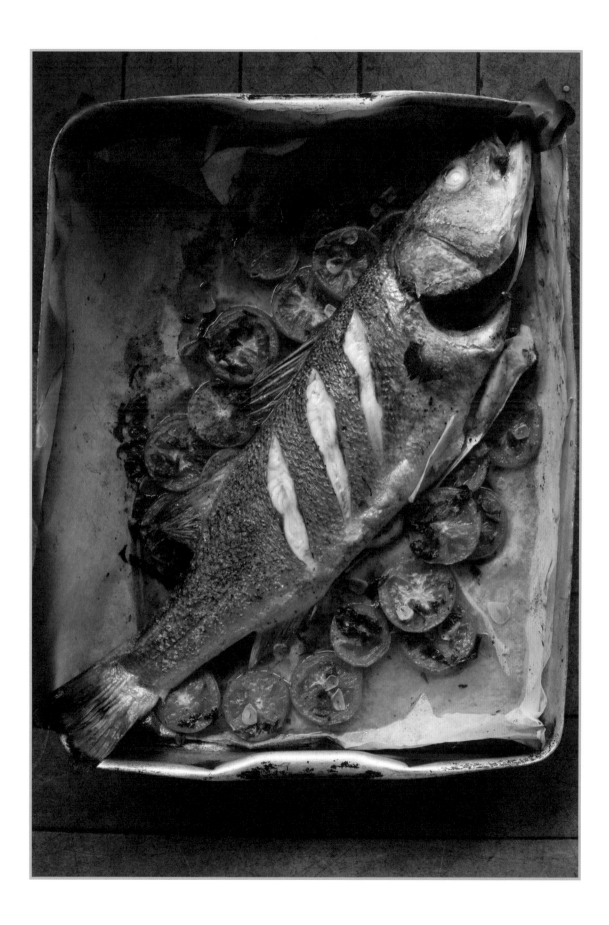

BIG PORTUGUESE FISH STEW

CALDEIRADA DE MARISCOS JORGE CARDOSO

SERVES 6

Almost every restaurant on the Cascais/Estoril coast has some kind of fish *caldeirada*. The combination of fish used depends on what's available, so modify the suggestions below if you have to.

18 raw king prawns
about 40 large mussels
2 onions, finely chopped
3 garlic cloves, finely chopped
4 tablespoons olive oil
2 bay leaves
a pinch of saffron
2 green and 2 red peppers, cut into eighths
3 large baking potatoes, peeled and chopped
400g tin of peeled plum tomatoes, drained
   and chopped
1 tablespoon tomato purée
a pinch of hot paprika
100ml/3^1/$_2$fl oz white wine
500g/1lb 2oz monkfish cheeks or tail, cut
   into about 18 pieces
500g/1lb 2oz sea bass or sea bream, cleaned
   and cut into 3cm/1^1/$_4$-inch pieces
500g/1lb 2oz mackerel or sardines, cleaned
   and cut into 3cm/1^1/$_2$-inch pieces
salt and freshly ground black pepper
lemon halves, to serve

For the stock
1 celery stick, roughly chopped
1 carrot, roughly chopped
1 garlic clove, roughly chopped
1 bay leaf
3 peppercorns
1 litre/1^3/$_4$ pints water

Pull off the heads and shells of the prawns and set aside. Remove the black vein from the back of each prawn with the tip of a knife. Put the heads and shells in a pan with all the ingredients for the stock and bring to the boil. After 3 minutes, lower the heat to a simmer and cook for a further 45 minutes, skimming off the scum with a ladle. Pour the stock through a sieve and set aside.

Scrub the mussels, removing any barnacles and their beards and throwing away any open ones that won't close when tapped on a work surface. In a large saucepan, gently fry the onions and garlic in the olive oil until softened. Add the bay leaves and saffron and fry until the onions are light brown. Add the pepper and potatoes and fry for 3 minutes, then stir in the tomatoes and cook for a further 3 minutes. Add 750ml/1^1/$_4$ pints of the hot stock, plus the tomato purée, paprika and wine. Boil for 3 minutes and then reduce to a medium heat. If you want a thicker consistency, break up some of the potato pieces with the back of a spoon. Season with salt and pepper to taste.

Increase the heat and add the monkfish and prawns, then 2 minutes later, add the bass or bream and mussels. After a further 2 minutes add the mackerel or sardines and turn off the heat. The mackerel or sardines will cook in the residual heat. Serve in large bowls, with halved lemons.

OCTOPUS STEW
WITH SPICES FROM GOA

TOM NORRINGTON-DAVIES

SERVES 6

Recheado is a spicy, red paste from the former Portuguese enclave of Goa. It is a sort of Indian cousin to Piri-Piri (see page 110). *Recheado* can be used as a marinade or even a stuffing for grilled fish. In this recipe it forms the base of a rich stew. You can make this a day ahead of eating it: a trick that does wonders for all 'curries', as the flavours intensify overnight. Serve the finished dish over rice or, even better, potatoes.

2 or 3 medium-sized octopus (around
500g/1lb 2oz each)
3 tablespoons olive oil
2 onions, roughly chopped
2 or 3 red or green peppers
a glass of white wine
1 teaspoon sugar
a bunch of fresh coriander, roughly chopped
salt and freshly ground black pepper

For the recheado
1 teaspoon cumin seeds
2 tablespoons dried red chillies
1 cinnamon stick, broken up
1 teaspoon cloves
1 teaspoon cardamom pods
3 bay leaves
2 tablespoons smoked paprika
1 tablespoon olive oil
1 onion, finely chopped
4 or 5 garlic cloves, finely chopped
1 teaspoon salt
100ml/3½fl oz white wine vinegar

First make the *recheado*: heat a heavy-bottomed frying pan, throw in all the spices and give them a dry roasting on the hob for about a minute, until you smell them unlocking their flavours. It is obvious when this happens. Transfer the spices to a food processor or blender and grind them

thoroughly. Heat the oil in the same pan and fry the onion and garlic until tender. Add them to the ground spices with the salt and vinegar and blend again until you have a smooth paste. If it seems too stiff, add a little more oil.

Here is how to attack a whole octopus: lay it flat on the chopping board with the tentacles to the right. Remove them with a sharp knife and keep to one side. Where the tentacles meet the body is the head. You should be able to see the eyes. Octopuses have no bones but there is a hard, shell-like beak. Cut the beak and eyes away and discard them. The body will contain all sorts of gunk, and is best cleaned by turning it inside out, like a rubber glove. Then you can wash everything away. What you are left with (the tentacles and body) can be cut up like a pepper or sliced into rings.

Heat the oil in a large pan and fry the onions and peppers in it until tender. Add the octopus and a generous tablespoon of the *recheado* paste (the rest can be stored in the fridge in a tightly sealed jar, where it should keep for ages). Turn the heat up high and stir thoroughly. Add the wine and let it bubble fiercely. Cover the pan, lower the heat and cook gently for 1½–2 hours or until the octopus is very tender. Check the stew often to make sure that it doesn't dry out. If it does, add a little water. Stir in the sugar and some salt and pepper, plus more *recheado* if you want more heat. But be careful if leaving it to rest overnight; it may become hotter by itself – chillies have a way of doing this.

Serve the stew on mounds of rice, with the coriander sprinkled on top, or with lots of bread.

ABOUT SALT COD

A good fishmonger should stock salt cod, or be able to get it for you. You can also find it in delicatessens and even some supermarkets. Buy salt cod that is as thick as possible, without any yellowing, which happens when it has been badly stored. Wash as much salt from the fish as you can and then soak it, skin side up, in plenty of cold water in the fridge for a day or so. Change the water two or three times during this period. Even better, and quicker, would be to have a constant flow of water running over the fish, although I admit this is hardly feasible in an average kitchen. The fish should not taste overly salty at the end of the soaking period; the only way to check it is to taste a bit.

Some recipes ask that the flesh is removed from the bones at this stage; others require you to poach the fish first. In the latter case, bring a large pan of water to a barely moving simmer, add the cod and cook for 15–20 minutes, until it begins to flake. Drain the fish and remove any bones and skin.

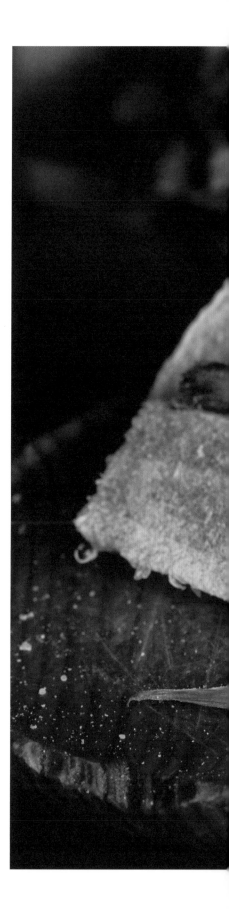

ESQUEIXADA
SAM & SAM CLARK

This is a classic Spanish salt cod salad from the Catalan region and it is often served as tapas. The essential part of this recipe is to shred the cod as Esqueixada comes from the Spanish verb *esqueixar*, meaning to shred.

300g thick fillet salt cod (dry weight), washed and soaked in cold water in the fridge for 48 hours, changing the water 4 times
1 green pepper, halved, deseeded and thinly sliced
1 red pepper, halved, deseeded and thinly sliced
15 cherry tomatoes, halved
1 large bunch fresh flat-leaf parsley, roughly chopped
½ small red onion, sliced wafer-thin
a handful of small black or green olives (such as arbequina *or* niçoise)

For the dressing
½ garlic clove
1½ tablespoons red wine vinegar
4 tablespoons extra virgin olive oil
sea salt and freshly ground black pepper

Drain the salt cod and remove any skin or bones. Shred the cod between your fingers into soft, fibrous flakes. Transfer to a mixing bowl and add the peppers, tomatoes, half the parsley and the onion.

For the dressing, crush the garlic with ½ teaspoon of salt to a paste, using a pestle and mortar. Whisk the garlic paste, vinegar and olive oil together, then season with pepper. Pour over the salt cod and gently toss together. Cover and refrigerate for about 1 hour.

Serve the salad with the remaining parsley and the olives sprinkled on top.

SALT COD WITH PRUNES AND PICKLING ONIONS

BACCALÀ ALLA PALMERITANA FULVIA MARCONI

SERVES 4

The sweet and sour flavours of this Sicilian salt cod stew are a reminder of the Arabic influences of Sicily. My grandmother always cooked this dish for Christmas Eve.

4 tablespoons olive oil
1 onion, finely chopped
750g/1lb 10oz salt cod, soaked (see page 122)
250g/9oz tomatoes (tinned or fresh), chopped
100g/4oz prunes
200g/7oz pickling onions (you can use cipollini – silverskin onions – or the white bulbs from spring onions), peeled but left whole
salt and freshly ground black pepper

Heat the oil in a heavy pan, add the onion and cook until lightly browned. Add the soaked and drained salt cod, then cover and leave for 10 minutes over a medium heat. Add the tomatoes and prunes and simmer gently for 20 minutes, then add the pickling onions. Cook for 30 minutes more on a very gentle heat, until the pickling onions are tender. Carefully stir in some seasoning, then serve. Buon appetito!

BAKED SALT COD WITH PEPPERS AND POTATOES BACALHAU COM BATATAS

PAULO SANTOS

SERVES 6

This was one of the first dishes I saw being cooked at the Eagle – the smell of the salt cod, peppers, onions and potatoes took me back home to Brazil. It is sometimes called by the Lisboan slang name, bacalhauada. The flavours complement each other really well.

800g/1³/₄lb dried salt cod, soaked
  (see page 122)
6 tablespoons olive oil, plus extra for
  drizzling
2 large Spanish onions, sliced
4 garlic cloves, finely chopped
2 green peppers, sliced
12 large Cyprus potatoes, peeled and
  quartered
2 bay leaves
juice of 1 lemon
2 handfuls of chopped parsley
4 tablespoons black olives
3 vine-ripened tomatoes, sliced
3 hard-boiled eggs, sliced
freshly grated black pepper

Put the soaked salt cod in a large saucepan of simmering water and cook gently for 15–20 minutes, until the flesh is beginning to flake. Drain and leave to cool a little – pick out any bones while it is still warm. Toss the fish with a couple of tablespoons of the oil to keep it warm.

Fry the onions in the remaining oil until soft and brown, then add the garlic and green peppers and cook for 2–3 minutes.

Meanwhile, in a separate pan, cover the potatoes with salted cold water, bring to the boil and simmer for 5 minutes. Drain them and add them to the onion and peppers. Add the bay leaves, lemon juice, half the parsley, the salt cod and some black pepper and mix carefully. Transfer the mixture to a baking dish and cook in an oven preheated to 200°C/gas mark 6 for 30 minutes. Remove from the oven and sprinkle over the olives and tomatoes. Cook for a further 5 minutes, then put the sliced hard-boiled eggs on top, sprinkle with the remaining parsley and drizzle with olive oil. Serve hot, with a bowl of green salad.

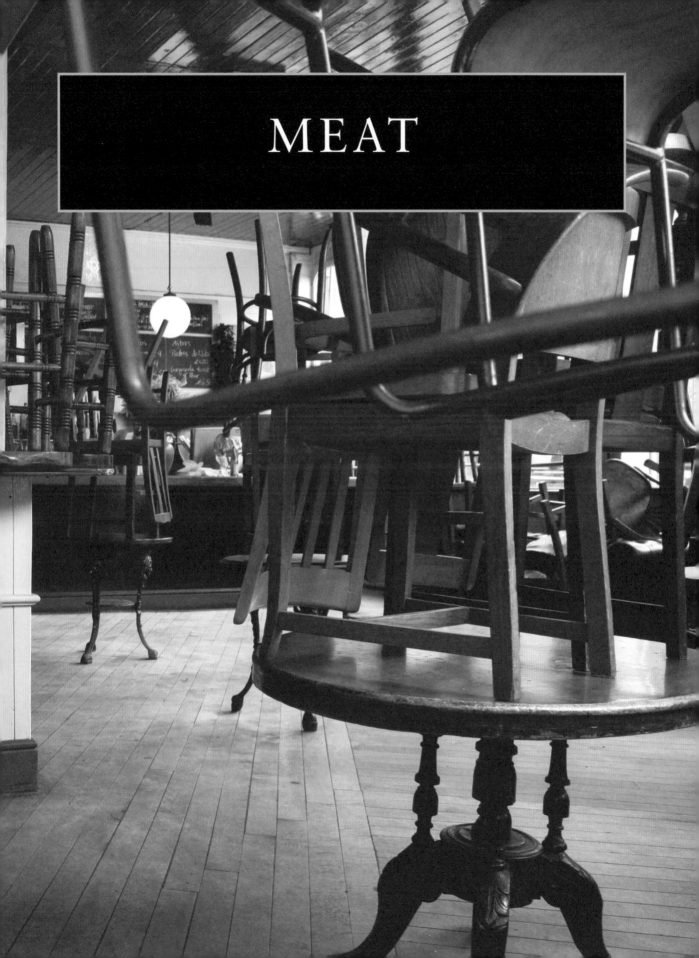

MEAT

ABOUT GRILLING MEAT

The centre of the Eagle's very small and open kitchen is the well-used chargrill. At times, more than half the menu's dishes include at least one component that has been cooked on the grill, and consequently much of our reputation for big flavours and rough edges should be attributed to it. Now, in an ideal world, the grill would be fired by charcoal and not by gas and lava rocks, for the reason that food cooked over glowing coals just tastes better. So we should all be happy that the barbecues we have at home are really the best thing on which to grill food (even if it may not be everyone's desire to fire up the barbecue for a couple of veal chops for their tea). That said, a barbecue should have a much larger surface area than the food being grilled is likely to occupy; the perimeter, where the heat is less intense, is useful for slowing things down or for resting them after cooking. The next best thing to using a barbecue is a large, rectangular, ridged cast iron grill pan – the type that uses two adjacent burners on your stove.

When grilling cuts of meat that have an element of fat – chops and most steaks – a medium heat is best. Salt the fat only and lightly oil the meat (not the grill bars, which serves no purpose), then start with the fat and any bone nearer to the hotter parts (salt helps to draw out water and lets the more volatile fats melt quickly, leaving the more robust fat to crisp up). Turn the meat 90 degrees halfway through cooking the first side and salt when turning it. Halfway through cooking the second side, turn again and move the meat to where the heat is lowest to complete the grilling. This will prevent it inadvertently overcooking and, as with roasts, will allow it to relax a little. Any bones will have warmed up and the meat near them will have cooked.

Lean cuts – chicken breasts, fillet steak, goat, venison and the like – require steady cooking on a higher heat but only until done to a degree before you want them. Then rest for 5–10 minutes in a warm spot to finish. If you don't rest meat, the result will be unevenly cooked and probably tough. Thin slices such as calf's liver can be cooked all the way on the hottest part of the grill without resting.

Duck breasts are an extreme example. On one side there is very lean meat with no fat at all and on the other a thick layer of fat that needs to be rendered crisp. So start with the salted and scored fatty side on the lowest heat available and cook until the fat is toasty brown. Turn the breast and now cook fiercely and briefly to rare, then leave to rest in a warm spot until pink throughout.

You may have noticed that chefs are forever prodding grilling meat with their forefinger. This is simply to ascertain the degree of 'doneness' and it is the only really practical method; thermometers are fine when testing roasts but not much good for smaller cuts. In general, a rare cut such as steak will feel much like the edge of your palm below the little finger; medium rare like the fleshy part of your palm at the base of the thumb; and medium like the centre of your palm. It takes some practice, but that is the way I test for doneness.

ABOUT ROASTING MEAT

The basic techniques for roasting meat successfully are logical enough. If the cut is lean, I would tend to seal the outside all over by either frying it or starting the roasting in a hot oven and then lowering the temperature for the final period of cooking. Conversely, a fattier cut of meat or bird might benefit from initial roasting in a moderate oven to start the fat running and then at a higher oven temperature for the last 30 minutes or so to crisp it up.

Lean joints of beef or veal are often barded with pork fat or rolled and tied with a thin layer of fat to prevent them becoming too dry. However, avoid lean birds that are advertised as 'self-basting', as they have probably been injected with animal fats in order to lubricate otherwise dry and tasteless meat. I prefer most joints to have the bone still attached whenever possible, as I think they taste better, although they will take longer to cook – the bone takes longer to heat up sufficiently to cook the surrounding meat – so the roasting has to be done at a lower temperature.

I have always believed that precise cooking times cannot be adhered to on account of all the variables: the difference between ovens, the position of the roast in the oven, the cut, the size of any bones, the density of the meat, and so on. Besides, the gradations on thermostat knobs are never more than approximate. So faithfully following recipes that recommend you to cook for 20 minutes per pound at such and such a temperature will often lead to failure. I generally check the roast by cutting into it and seeing if the juices are beginning to run clear, which would indicate that it is at the medium-rare stage.

Even better, invest in a meat thermometer, which tells you the temperature at the centre of the roast. More primitive – but, with practice, just as successful – is the chef's trick of pushing a steel skewer into the meat, counting to ten before removing it and then touching the tip to your lip. If it is barely warm, then the meat is medium rare. Blood temperature is rare.

Never serve a roast straight from the oven. Instead, cook it to a degree before you want it, then let it rest for 20 minutes in a warm place, covered in foil, shiny side in (or leave it in the turned-off oven), to cook through. The meat will relax and become more tender. In the case of beef or lamb, it will be uniformly pink inside if removed from the oven when rare. The juices that run into the pan while the meat is resting can be used to dress the roast or become the basis of a gravy.

A word also on domestic ovens. They rarely have the necessary capacity or power to maintain a constant high temperature, so don't expect a 5.5kg/12lb goose to cook evenly if it only just fits into the oven. Fan-assisted ovens overcome this problem, as they help keep all parts of the oven at the same temperature. If your oven is not so equipped, preheat it for at least 30 minutes to a higher temperature than needed, then turn the thermostat down to the required temperature as the roast is put in and keep your checks on it to a minimum.

STEAK SANDWICH

BIFE ANA DAVID EYRE

This has to be in this book; it's the only dish to have been on the menu at the Eagle every single day since we opened. When notions of having a pub first arose, a steak sandwich was just about the first item to appear on the business plan's menu. Not just any steak sandwich, but the one I remembered eating almost daily whilst a teenager home on school holidays in Mozambique.

Not to be confused with the Portuguese fried pork escalope of the same name, this (beef) steak sandwich is named after Dona Ana, a larger-than-life mafiosa who owned a cattle ranch, bakery and bar. The bakery and ranch provided the primary ingredients for the huge *pregos* – the real (Portuguese) name – served in the bar.

500g/1lb 2oz rump steak, thinly sliced (the
  original would have used fillet)
2 large crusty rolls – we use stone-baked
  Portuguese rolls called carcaças
2 tablespoons olive oil
Cos lettuce leaves
salt

For the marinade
1 onion, thinly sliced
1 garlic clove, chopped
1 small dried chilli, crushed
1 bay leaf, broken up
1 tablespoon chopped parsley
1 teaspoon dried oregano
2 tablespoons red wine
3 tablespoons olive oil
freshly ground black pepper

Mix together all the ingredients for the marinade, add the steak and leave to marinate for a few hours (but no longer than 8 hours). Remove the steaks from the marinade, then strain it and set aside.

Warm the rolls in a medium oven. Heat a heavy-based frying pan until very, very hot, then add the olive oil and fry the steaks very quickly. If your pan is hot enough, they will need to be turned within a minute. Remove the steaks and keep warm, then add the dry ingredients from the marinade to the pan with some salt.

Cut the rolls in half and arrange the Cos lettuce and then the steaks on the lower halves. Add the strained marinade liquid to the pan and let this bubble and reduce a little, then pour into the top halves of the rolls. Close the sandwiches and eat immediately, with both hands.

SADDLE OF LAMB
STUFFED WITH TAPENADE

AMANDA PRITCHETT

Ask your butcher to bone the saddle of lamb and leave it untied. It's best to stuff it a few hours before you roast it to let the flavours seep in. The quantities given below for the tapenade make a large jar, which will keep well if you cover it with olive oil and store it in the fridge. Use for grilled fish or meat.

1 saddle of lamb (without the chump)
4 tablespoons olive oil
salt and freshly ground black pepper

For the tapenade
about 500g/1lb 2oz black olives, pitted
3 garlic cloves, chopped
juice of 1 large lemon
150ml/¹/₄ pint olive oil
a handful of capers, soaked in cold water
  for 30 minutes and then squeezed
¹/₂ small tin of anchovies, drained
1 heaped teaspoon Dijon mustard
a shot of brandy

Put all the ingredients for the tapenade in a food processor and pulse until the mixture is nearly smooth but still retains some texture.

Put the saddle skin-side down and open it out. Spread about 4 tablespoons of the tapenade on to and into all the surfaces of the meat. Fold it up and turn it over. You will need to tie it up. First tie a piece of string around the whole thing horizontally and then a few pieces in a row perpendicular to the first string. The tapenade will do most of the seasoning but lightly salt and pepper the outside of the meat. Set aside for a few hours so it can absorb the flavours of the tapenade.

Heat the olive oil in a roasting tin on the hob and brown the saddle all over. Transfer to an oven, preheated to 200°C/gas mark 6 and roast for about 45 minutes. To check if the meat is done, insert a skewer right into the centre and leave it for 10 seconds, then lay it on your lips; it should be blood temperature. Leave the meat to rest in a warm place for 20–30 minutes, then carve into thick slices and serve with roast potatoes and French beans or salad.

COLD RARE BEEF FILLET
FILETTO FREDDO **KATE LEWIS**

SERVES 4

If you like rare beef, this is one of the most delicious and simple ways to eat it. The meat is grilled to a crust and roasted very briefly, then allowed to rest for at least 30 minutes. There is something very special about having a piece of fillet on your board and preparing it in such a simple way that the quality of the meat speaks for itself – it is just the best cut of beef available. At the Eagle we are lucky enough to use the whole fillet – a rare sight for most domestic cooks, but well worth it if you're cooking for a crowd.

In terms of both quality and expense, I would advise you to buy fillet from your local butcher – supermarket prices make this dish exorbitant.

1kg/2¼lb beef fillet
a little olive oil
sea salt and freshly ground black pepper

Trim any fat off the fillet. Lightly oil it and roll it in plenty of coarsely ground black pepper. Heat a grill or griddle pan to very hot and season the fillet well with salt. Grill on all sides until a crust forms (2–3 minutes per side). Place on a hot baking tray and roast on the top shelf of an oven preheated to 200°C/gas mark 6 for 3–6 minutes, depending on whether you have the thin (tail) end or the thick end of the fillet. Remove the beef from the oven and leave to rest for at least 30 minutes before cutting it into thin slices and sprinkling over more salt.

Serve with hot new potatoes and salsa verde.

SALSA VERDE
This raw parsley sauce is traditionally served in Italy with boiled meats, but it makes a pleasant sharp foil for any cold cuts or grills. You have to chop all the ingredients separately with a good chef's knife, otherwise the result will be a kind of pesto. The proportions are not that important: you'll need a measuring jug filled to the 500ml/18fl oz mark with chopped flat-leaf parsley (curly English parsley won't do), with (or without) other sweet herbs such as tarragon, mint, basil, chervil and chives; 5 anchovy fillets; 2 tablespoons of capers; 2 tablespoons of small gherkins; a teaspoon of (preferably fresh) horseradish or mustard; and a tablespoon of red wine vinegar. Chop everything finely, mix together and stir in about 150ml/¼ pint of olive oil; the sauce should be runny and spoonable rather than a thick paste. Taste and adjust the seasoning if necessary.

ROAST PORK, TUSCAN STYLE

ARISTA DAVID EYRE

SERVES 6–8

This Tuscan pork loin roast with garlic and fennel seed has never failed me. The dry marinade subtly perfumes the meat and somehow prevents the pork drying out. The loin is normally prepared with the skin removed, which certainly helps in the marinating process. In Italy all the skin seems to be saved for use in their very fine sausages. Thus crackling is unknown, which is a shame as surely that's the whole point of roast pork. Ask your butcher to leave the bone on the loin but loosened from the meat to make carving easier. Ask, too, that the roast be cut from the rib end of the loin and, if you want the crackling, for the skin to be scored and removed – it can be roasted alongside.

5 garlic cloves, chopped
2 tablespoons fennel seeds
3 tablespoons chopped parsley
2 teaspoons salt
fruity olive oil
1 pork loin weighing 2–3kg/4$\frac{1}{2}$–6$\frac{1}{2}$lb,
*   prepared as described above*
freshly ground black pepper

In a food processor or pestle and mortar, grind together the garlic, fennel seeds, parsley, salt and some freshly ground black pepper, then mix in enough olive oil to make a paste. Rub this thoroughly all over the meat and tie the meat up with string. If you can leave it in the fridge overnight, all the better.

Roast uncovered in an oven preheated to 180°C/gas mark 4 for about 1$\frac{1}{2}$ hours, then turn the oven up high and continue roasting for half and hour or so. A meat thermometer in the centre of the joint should read 80C. To make crackling, rub plenty of salt (but no oil) into the skin and roast separately – remove from the oven if it is done before the meat is ready.

Leave the meat to rest for 20 minutes or so, then carve it into thick slices and serve with any form of Oven Potatoes (see page 184) and perhaps Roast Red Onions (see page 168).

ROAST CHICKEN WITH TARRAGON, GARLIC AND OLIVES DAVID EYRE

SERVES 4

There is nothing like tarragon, olives and garlic for elevating a humble roast chicken in a south-west France manner. Choose a medium-sized, organic or decent free-range roasting chicken, which may well be costly – I really think that we've become used to thinking of chicken as everyday food, when really it should be more special than that. Don't bother with the small, meritless poussins, or spring chickens, as they invariably lack flavour. 'Black leg' chickens (also known as *poulet noir* if imported from France) are a favourite at the Eagle for roasting. Some supermarkets and good butcher's shops now stock them.

a 1.5kg/3¼lb roasting chicken
rind and juice of 1 lemon
4 garlic cloves, roughly chopped
1 streaky bacon rasher, finely chopped
1 heaped tablespoon chopped tarragon
about 20 black olives, pitted and roughly chopped
2 tablespoons olive oil
coarse sea salt and freshly ground black pepper

Wash the bird well and dry it thoroughly. Rub it all over with coarse sea salt, pepper and lemon rind, working it under the skin and into the body cavity. Mix the garlic with the chopped bacon, tarragon and olives and put it all into the cavity. Squeeze the lemon juice over the bird and rub it in with the olive oil. Place in a roasting tin, breast side up, and wrap it loosely, but airtight, with foil. Roast in an oven preheated to 180°C/gas mark 4 for about 35 minutes (this method keeps the meat moist), then remove the foil, baste the chicken and cook at 220°C/gas mark 7 for 20 minutes or more to crisp it up. The juices from a cut made in the thick part of the thigh should run clear when the bird is ready. Leave to rest for 10 minutes, then pour off the juices and carve the chicken. Eat with potatoes of some kind or simple rice.

GRILLED CHICKEN BREASTS WITH OREGANO, LEMON AND BLACK PEPPER DAVID EYRE

SERVES 4

Chicken breasts simply grilled and served with some form of leaf and herb salad are always going to be a favourite. Whether grilled on a ridged pan for a mid-week supper or on the barbecue at the weekend, this is all about giving a dull chicken breast some big flavours. Chicken breasts need to be cooked steadily on a medium heat; the aim is that the breast meat should not be dry by the time the meat around the wing bone is just cooked.

4 large (225–250g/8–9oz) free-range chicken
 breasts
2 tablespoons finely chopped fresh oregano
 (or marjoram) – you could use dried for a
 different result, but use less than half the
 quantity
3 tablespoons olive oil
1 small dried chilli, crushed
more freshly ground black pepper then you
 would expect – about 1 level tablespoon
2 lemons
sea salt

Wash and dry the chicken breasts. Mix with the oregano, oil, chilli, black pepper and the grated zest of one of the lemons and leave to marinate whilst the grill heats up or the charcoal dies down to an even medium heat. When ready to cook, salt the chicken and squeeze one of the lemons all over it. Cook the breasts, turning them 90 degrees once on each side, then remove from the heat. Squeeze the juice of the other lemon over them, sprinkle with a little more olive oil and leave to rest for a moment. If you happen to have some truffle oil, now is the time to make good use of it. Serve with a mixed leaf salad containing chives, parsley and spring onions.

GRILLED FENNEL SAUSAGES, LENTILS AND GREEN SAUCE

TOM NORRINGTON-DAVIES

Italian delis often supply a range of coarse sausages, usually bound with old-fashioned butchers string. Those seasoned with fennel are fantastic. Serving them with lentils and salsa verde is a classic eagle treatment. Because of their coarse texture, Italian sausages are ideal for braising but can burst when grilled or fried. This is best avoided by a quick blanching trick, which we will talk you through.

170g puy lentils
6 tablespoons extra virgin olive oil
1 onion, thinly sliced
1 fennel bulb, thinly sliced
1 leek, thinly sliced
2 cloves of garlic
1 glass white wine
juice of 1 lemon
1 tablespoon of Dijon mustard
salt and freshly ground black pepper
12 fennel sausages, cut from their strings
4–6 tablespoons salsa verde (green sauce, see page 135 for recipe)

Cook the lentils first. Heat the oil in a saucepan and gently cook all the vegetables and the garlic until soft, then add the lentils. Add the wine and reduce. Cover in water and cook for about 20–30 minutes. Try to avoid them turning to mush, they should hold their shape but not be crunchy. Finish with a squeeze of lemon, a dollop of mustard, an extra splash of olive oil and season to taste. Allow the lentils to sit in a warm place while you cook the sausages. They won't take long.

Preheat an overhead or stove top, ridged grilling pan. Pop the sausages into a saucepan and just cover them with cold, unsalted water. Bring the water to scalding point and, before they boil, drain the sausages immediately. Transfer the sausages to the grill or griddle pan and cook them until they are well marked all over, and fully cooked (about four minutes each side).

Serve the sausages on top of the lentils with the salsa verde and, if you like, lots of bread for mopping.

GRILLED LEG OF VENISON
TRISH HILFERTY

SERVES 10

This is something a bit different to do with venison – a meat that not long ago was considered a luxury but is now a fairly affordable option. It has started to gain popularity, probably due to its lack of fat. This does make it susceptible to dryness if it is overcooked. Aim for rare and juicy with this one. Perfect for a posh barbecue.

2–2.5kg/4¹/₂–5¹/₂lb leg of venison (boned and trimmed weight)
4 garlic cloves, crushed
100ml/3¹/₂fl oz olive oil
a handful of rosemary and thyme, chopped
freshly ground black pepper

First you need to butterfly the leg of venison. Slice through the thinnest part of the boned leg – the underside – then open it up and flatten out. Trim off any sinew and slash through the larger muscles to give a more uniform thickness for even cooking.

Put the flattened leg in a glass or ceramic dish. Mix together the garlic, oil, herbs and some black pepper to make a marinade and pour it over the meat, massaging it in well. Cover and refrigerate for about 8 hours or overnight, turning occasionally.

Bring the meat back to room temperature. Season with sea salt and another grinding of pepper. Heat a barbecue or large chargrill pan to the highest point. Slap on the meat and leave till brown and crisp, then turn, doing the same for the other side. Reduce the heat and cook slowly for 30 minutes. It is important that the heat is reduced or the meat will burn on the outside and be raw in the middle. Leave to rest on a warm plate, loosely covered, for about 20 minutes before carving.

VENISON AND PANCETTA CASSEROLE

RUTH QUINLAN

SERVES 8

This is a rich, gamey winter stew. Get the butcher to bone the venison for you. Buy your pancetta or bacon at the butcher's too, then cut the rind off and use it to give the stew juices extra flavour. Serve with Celeriac Mash (see page 180).

2 tablespoons vegetable oil
200g/7oz pancetta or streaky bacon,
  without rind, chopped into small pieces
1 shoulder of venison (about 1.5kg/3¼lb),
  boned, cut into chunks and sprinkled with
  salt
½ bottle of red wine
2 onions, chopped
2 carrots, cut into small dice
2 leeks, finely sliced
3 celery sticks, finely sliced
2 garlic cloves, finely chopped, and 4 whole
  cloves, peeled
a few parsley stalks, finely chopped
3 tablespoons olive oil
1 tablespoon tomato purée
1 bunch of thyme, tied
salt and freshly ground black pepper

Heat the vegetable oil in a large frying pan, add the pancetta and fry until browned. Take the pancetta out of the pan, then brown the venison in the same fat, a few pieces at a time. Put all the browned meat in a casserole dish. Pour a slosh of the wine into the frying pan and scrape up any meaty bits that may have stuck to the bottom. Pour this over the meat. Gently fry the vegetables, chopped garlic, whole garlic cloves and parsley stalks in the olive oil for 15 minutes, then add the tomato purée, thyme, the rest of the red wine and the bacon rind. Pour this mixture over the meat. Add sufficient water to half submerge the meat. Dip your finger into the liquid to taste and then adjust the seasoning as necessary. Cook, covered, for 2 hours at 160°C/gas mark 3, until tender.

VEAL OR CHICKEN WITH TUNA DRESSING VITELLO O CAPONE TONNATO

TRISH HILFERTY

SERVES 6

There are as many recipes for *vitello tonnato* as there are Italian chefs. This one offers a nod to cookery writer Marcella Hazan. It is the perfect party dish, as all the preparation can be done well in advance.

Capons are castrated male chickens – a process that was practised for centuries to obtain a heavier, plumper bird. When Paris welcomed Catherine de Medici in 1549 , the sumptuous banquet given in her honour included 43 *capons*. However, castrating chickens is now illegal, so just use the biggest free-range chicken you can find.

1 large chicken, or 1 topside of veal
 weighing 1.5kg/3¹/₄lb, trimmed of fat
 and tied
1 head garlic, cloves separated and chopped
3 celery sticks, chopped
2 small onions, chopped
2 carrots, chopped
2 bay leaves
a sprig of thyme
4 black peppercorns
a pinch of salt

For the dressing
2 egg yolks
2 teaspoons Dijon mustard
300ml/¹/₂ pint olive oil
125g/4¹/₂oz good-quality tuna in oil
8 anchovies, chopped, plus a few extra
 to decorate
1 tablespoon capers, plus a few extra
 to decorate, soaked in cold water for
 30 minutes and then squeezed
juice of ¹/₂ lemon
salt and freshly ground black pepper

If using chicken, put it in a large pot with the garlic, vegetables and herbs and pour in just enough water to cover. Add the peppercorns and salt and bring slowly to a simmer. Cook gently for 20 minutes, then take off the heat and cover loosely. Leave the chicken to cool completely in the stock; it will finish cooking as it cools.

If you are using veal, put it in a large pot with the garlic, vegetables and herbs and pour in enough water to cover. Remove the veal, bring the water to the boil, then return the veal to the pot, adding the peppercorns and salt. Bring to a simmer and cook gently for 1¹/₄ hours. Take off the heat and leave the meat to cool completely in the liquid.

Make the dressing as for mayonnaise: put the egg yolks, mustard, a pinch of salt and a good grinding of pepper in a good processor or blender and mix well. With the machine running, add the oil slowly at first, gradually adding it faster as the mayonnaise becomes emulsified. Beat in the tuna along with its oil, the chopped anchovies and capers. Add the lemon juice and adjust the seasoning. The finished mayonnaise should have a coating consistency. If it is too thick, add a little stock.

To assemble the dish, remove the meat from the cooking liquid. With the chicken, pull all the flesh from the carcass – this isn't a neatly carved affair. Slice the veal fairly thinly. Spread half the dressing on a large plate. Arrange the meat in a single layer on top, then coat with the remaining dressing. If possible, leave it for an hour to allow the flavours to mingle. Strew the extra capers and anchovies over your finished dish. Eat it with a big green salad, crusty bread and a bottle of rosé.

MUTTON CHOP AND POTATO HOTPOT
MARGOT HENDERSON

A fantastic all-in-one dish – easy to prepare and full of flavour. Serve simply with steamed carrots or Savoy cabbage.

12 mutton chops, with kidneys attached
115g/4oz plain flour
4 tablespoon olive oil
4 onions, finely chopped
4 garlic cloves, finely chopped
2 leeks, finely sliced
1¹/₂kg/3¹/₄lb waxy potatoes, e.g. Maris Peer
  or Estima, sliced into 5mm/¹/₄-inch rounds
1.2 litres/2 pints chicken stock
salt and freshly ground black pepper
steamed carrots or Savoy cabbage, to serve

Preheat the oven to 200°C/gas mark 6.

Season the flour with salt and freshly ground black pepper. Dust the chops with a little of the seasoned flour. Heat half the oil in a large heavy-based pan over a medium-high heat and brown the chops in batches, set aside.

Add the remaining oil to the pan and cook the onions, garlic and leeks over a medium heat until soft.

Place a layer of the potato slices into a large casserole dish. Then add a layer of chops and a layer of the vegetable mix. Repeat the layers, seasoning between them and finishing with a layer of potatoes.

Cover with a lid and cook for 40 minutes. Uncover for the last 10 minutes of the cooking time to brown the potatoes. Serve with carrots or cabbage.

LAMB SHANKS WITH CHICKPEAS
TOM NORRINGTON-DAVIES

A dish for patient people. The key to tasty lamb shanks and soft chickpeas is time, lots of it. The meat should be cooked until it is almost falling off the bone; the chickpeas should be creamy, with very little bite. This dish is quite brothy – the stock pretty much makes itself, due to the long cooking processes.

5 tablespoons olive oil
6 lamb shanks
2 large onions, roughly chopped
3 garlic cloves, roughly chopped
3 leeks, roughly chopped
3 celery sticks, roughly chopped
about ¹/₂ bottle of white wine
1 teaspoon dried mint
a generous pinch of saffron
2 tablespoons tomato purée
about 250g/9oz chickpeas, soaked in cold
*   water overnight, or 2 x 400g/14oz tins of*
*   chickpeas (look for a brand that adds*
*   nothing but salt and water)*
a bunch of parsley or coriander, chopped
salt and freshly ground black pepper

Heat the olive oil in a large frying pan over a fierce heat. Brown the lamb shanks in it and then put them to one side. Pour the fat and juices from the pan into a large casserole and use them to fry the onions, garlic, leeks and celery, adding a little more oil if you need to. When the vegetables have softened but not browned, add the wine, mint and saffron. As soon as it is bubbling, stir in the tomato purée. Add the lamb shanks and turn to coat them with the other ingredients. Add enough water for the shanks to be just about covered, but not swimming. Cover and cook over a low heat for about 2 hours.

Meanwhile, deal with the chickpeas, if you are using dried ones. Drain them of their soaking water, put them in a large pan of unsalted water and bring to the boil. Boil them rapidly for 10 minutes, then drain again. Now cover them with fresh water again and simmer until tender. The best way to get chickpeas right is to keep tasting the odd one. If the water evaporates before the chickpeas are tender, just add more boiling water from the kettle.

When the lamb has been cooking for about 2 hours, add the chickpeas and enough of their cooking liquid to cover. If they look as if they will swamp the stew, don't add them all. Continue cooking until the lamb is tender and the chickpeas are a little overcooked; make sure the stew does not dry out – add a little more liquid if necessary.

Serve in bowls with plenty of liquid, garnished with the parsley or coriander and accompanied by some good bread for mopping up the juices.

PREPARING GLOBE ARTICHOKES

There are two things you must have to hand when preparing artichokes: a really sharp paring knife and a supply of halved lemons. The dark green, inedible parts of an artichoke are notoriously tough, and any cut surfaces will oxidise or blacken within a minute unless rubbed with lemon.

The simplest way to cook and eat an artichoke is to boil it in salted water containing a couple of lemon halves until the tip of a knife finds the heart or base to be tender (I don't like to cook them in anything other than stainless steel pans). First trim the tips of the petals by about a third and rub with lemon, then remove the first outer layer or so of the outer petals. Cut off the stem and carefully trim the remaining dark green bits from the base of the artichoke. Rub with lemon and put it in the saucepan. After cooking, open out the top of the artichoke and remove all of the hairy choke with a teaspoon (I use a worn, and thus sharp, one). To eat the artichoke, remove the leaves, each with a nugget of edible heart attached, and nibble this off until all that is left is the prize – the heart. Use a classic vinaigrette as a dip or sauce.

If you want to braise the artichokes or use them in a dish such as the Lamb, Olive and Artichoke Stew, opposite, then a little more work is needed. Snap off all the dark outer leaves until you are left with pale green ones; rub these with lemon. Cut off the top of the artichoke halfway down, remove the purple inner parts and the choke (all of it!) and rub with lemon. Trim the stem, leaving about 5cm/2 inches attached – less if the artichokes are large or not very fresh – then peel the woody outer layer of the stem. Again, lemon! Trim the remaining green parts as above. The artichoke can now be cut into slices or quarters, if large, not forgetting to rub them with more lemon. For the lamb stew I generally quarter them. Keep in water acidulated with the spent lemon halves until needed.

LAMB, OLIVE & ARTICHOKE STEW

PHIL PICKERING

SERVES 6

This Sardinian dish starts off with a *soffritto* – a mixture of finely chopped vegetables stewed gently in plenty of olive oil until tender. It's a classic Mediterranean technique that gives the stew a rich flavour base.

1 leg of lamb. boned and cut into 3cm/1¼–inch pieces, or cut into fist-sized chunks with the bone in
150ml/5fl oz olive oil
1 tablespoon tomato purée
400g/14oz tin of plum tomatoes, drained and chopped
a good bunch of flat-leaf parsley, leaves and stalks chopped separately
2 bay leaves
a glass of sherry or white wine
about 300ml/½ pint vegetable stock or water
20 kalamata olives, pitted
400g/14oz fresh globe artichokes, prepared (see opposite) – or, if you must, 2 tins of globe artichokes in brine, drained and rinsed
rind and juice of 2 lemons
salt and freshly ground black pepper

For the soffritto
3 onions, finely chopped
2 garlic cloves, finely chopped
2 carrots, finely chopped
2 celery sticks, finely chopped

In a large, heavy pan, fry the lamb in 3 tablespoons of the oil until browned all over. Drain, remove from the pan and set aside while you prepare the base for the stew. Pour off the fat from the pan, add the rest of the oil and sweat the *soffritto* vegetables in it with a pinch of salt and pepper for about 10 minutes, until the onions are glossy. Stir occasionally to keep them from sticking.

Add the tomato purée, plum tomatoes, parsley stalks, bay, the lamb, the sherry or wine and half the stock or water. Cover and simmer, stirring occasionally, for 50 minutes, or about 1½ hours if using lamb on the bone. The meat should be tender.

Skim away any fat from the surface by using the base of the ladle in a circular motion to spread the fat to one side, and then remove it. If necessary, add the rest of the stock or water to cover the meat. Now add the olives, artichokes and the rest of the parsley and heat gently for 10 minutes. Squeeze in the lemon juice, then taste for more salt and pepper to suit. Serve garnished with lemon rind and accompanied by rice, potatoes, mash or polenta.

BELLY PORK STEW WITH PEAS AND SAFFRON

TOM NORRINGTON-DAVIES

SERVES 6

This stew is from Galicia in northwest Spain, where a lot of vegetables are grown because of the wetter climate. Although we often make pork stews at the Eagle, this one doesn't appear on the menu very often because of the peas, which we tend to cook only in the summer. A word about peas: I am not shy of using frozen peas or broad beans in most dishes. Not only does it save time podding but the growers pack them so fresh that they often beat hands down the weary real McCoy arriving in London. If you have a garden and grow your own, that is, of course, another matter. The peas in this recipe are cooked for a long time so it may be prudent to use frozen peas anyway, saving your fresh ones for a chance to steal the show another day.
Our favourite cuts of pork for stewing at the Eagle are shoulder and belly, off the bone. We tend to use belly when there are other bulky ingredients such as beans or potatoes, since it is the fattiest cut. You may wish to trim the thick layer of fat (which makes crackling when you roast the meat) from either cut – it's entirely up to you.

4 tablespoons olive oil
1.5kg/3¼lb belly or shoulder of pork, boned and cut into large chunks
2 onions, finely chopped
3 garlic cloves, finely chopped
a glass of dry white wine
2 tablespoons sherry vinegar
a pinch of saffron
1 teaspoon tomato purée
1kg/2¼lb peas
3 large waxy potatoes, peeled and roughly chopped
a bunch of flat-leaf parsley, roughly chopped (about a handful)
salt and freshly ground black pepper

Heat half the olive oil in a large frying pan and brown the chunks of pork. This is a job best done in 2 or 3 batches. Be careful not to brown too many pieces at a time or they will stew rather than fry. When the pork is browned, put it to one side in a bowl to catch any escaping juices.

Gently heat the remaining oil in a large casserole and fry the onions and garlic until translucent and tender. Do not let them brown. Add the pork and its juices and stir briefly. Turn up the heat and add the wine and vinegar. When the wine is bubbling, add the saffron and tomato purée and stir thoroughly. Now turn the heat down low and let the stew reach a gentle simmer. Refill the wine glass with water and cover the meat with this. The pork should be just submerged enough to stew but not swim; add a little more water if necessary. Season with a pinch of black pepper and a good teaspoon of salt.

Cook gently until the pork is tender, which may take 1½–2 hours. About 30 minutes before serving, add the peas and potatoes and cook until the potatoes are tender but not falling apart. Check the seasoning again and serve in large bowls, garnished with the chopped parsley.

ASTURIAN PORK & BUTTERBEAN STEW FABADA ASTURIANA

DAVID EYRE

SERVES 8–10

It can be cold in northern Spain and they are famous in Asturias and Cantabria for their dried beans, which lend themselves to winter dishes. This is my favourite version of pork with beans. It uses large dried butter beans, known as *judiones* or simply *faves*, and seven different types of pork. I might occasionally include a pinch of saffron threads, added when all is gently boiling, but it would not be an authentic thing to do. It's a good idea to make this dish the day before eating it.

500g/1lb 2oz dried butter beans, soaked
    overnight in cold water
about 500g/1lb 2oz raw ham or gammon
    hock
1 raw pork hock or a trotter
500g/1lb 2oz streaky bacon in one piece,
    smoked or not
200g/7oz Spanish tocino (salted pork belly
    fat), Italian lardo salato, the fat trimmings
    from serrano or Parma ham, or really fat
    bacon
700g/1lb 9oz fresh belly pork, in slices, or
    veal shin in pieces (as would be cut for
    osso bucco)
4 bay leaves
a few sprigs of thyme
1 or 2 dried chillies
300g/11oz morcilla (Spanish blood sausage)
400g/14oz good-quality cooking chorizo
10 large garlic cloves, peeled
2 onions, sliced
salt and freshly ground black pepper

Put the drained beans and the hocks in a large pot, cover with cold water and boil for 15 minutes. Drain, then return to the pan and cover with hot water. Add the bacon, *tocino*, belly pork and herbs and cook for 1 hour at a steady simmer. Add the remaining ingredients and cook for another hour or until the beans are tender. Make sure that the stew is always just covered with water.

Remove the hocks and pick off the meat, then return it to the pot. Cut the bacon and chorizo into chunky pieces – the *morcilla* will have broken up. Check the seasoning but it is unlikely that salt will be needed. I sometimes stir in a handful of chopped flat-leaf parsley. Another good thing to eat with bread.

PORK & CLAMS, ALENTEJO STYLE
PORCO À ALENTEJANA DAVID EYRE

SERVES 6

Although it is from the south of the country, this dish is a great favourite with all Portuguese and, while the idea might sound a little wacky, I guarantee it will become a favourite of yours as well. It is typically cooked in a *cataplana* – a unique cooking vessel in the form of two copper bowls that are hinged rather like a giant clam shell – which can be used on the stove, in the oven or even in a fire. I invariably make it in a heavy saucepan with a tightly fitting lid. The Portuguese would use tiny clams but in my temperate island version I like to use well-washed cockles. You must fry the pork in lard or the flavour will not be right.

500g/1lb 2oz lean pork (leg or loin) cut into 2cm/³/₄-inch dice
500g/1lb 2oz belly pork, cut into 2cm/³/₄-inch dice
3–4 garlic cloves, finely chopped
1 heaped teaspoon paprika, preferably smoked
¹/₂ bottle of white wine
2 bay leaves
2 cloves
1kg/2¹/₄lb live cockles or small clams
125g/4¹/₂oz good-quality lard
75ml/2¹/₃fl oz olive oil
1 onion, finely chopped
3 tablespoons chopped parsley
1 generous tablespoon tomato purée
salt and freshly ground black pepper

Mix the meat with the garlic, paprika, wine, bay and cloves and leave to marinate for 3–6 hours. Scrub the cockles or clams well, throwing away any open ones that won't close when tapped. Leave them in a colander within a large pan or sink full of cold water to purge them of sand and grit. This may take several hours; shaking them about occasionally will speed things up.

Remove the pieces of meat from the marinade and strain it. Melt the lard in a large frying pan, add the meat, season with salt and pepper and fry steadily until nicely browned. You may have to do this in two batches. Pour the marinade into the pan and continue cooking the meat until it is tender – about half an hour.

Heat the olive oil in a separate pan and cook the onion in it with the parsley until softened. Stir in the tomato purée and simmer for 5 minutes, then add the cockles or clams. As soon as they have started to open, add the meat and cook, covered, for another 3–5 minutes. Check the seasoning and serve.

CASSEROLED BEEF WITH CINNAMON, THYME AND SHALLOTS DAVID EYRE

DAVID EYRE

SERVES 6–8

A rich beef stew in the classic manner. This method can be used with almost any appropriate ingredients. I can't remember where I came across cinnamon as something good for beef stews but its sweetness is very welcome. As for the shallots – well, beef and onions is a famous combination.
Possible additions or substitutions include olives, juniper berries and small white onions; brandy or more red wine could be used instead of the vinegar.

100g/4oz streaky bacon, chopped
100g/4oz salt pork fat (sold as lardo salato in Italian grocers), washed and chopped
1.5kg/3¼lb shin of beef, cut into 3cm/1¼-inch cubes
½ glass red wine vinegar
olive oil
10 shallots, peeled but left whole with the root intact (you may find it easier to peel them if they are soaked in cold water first)
5 fat garlic cloves, peeled but left whole
1 tablespoon tomato purée
a handful of flat-leaf parsley, chopped plus extra for garnish
2 fresh bay leaves
a large sprig of thyme
2 strips of orange peel
2 cinnamon sticks
2 glasses of strong red wine
water or meat stock
salt and freshly ground black pepper

Slowly melt the streaky bacon and pork fat in a wide, heavy casserole. Take the bacon out and put it in a warm bowl. Brown the beef in the pan – in batches if necessary – then add it to the bacon in the bowl. Pour the red wine vinegar into the hot pan and stir to deglaze, letting it bubble until slightly reduced. Pour it over the meat. Heat some olive oil in the pan, add the shallots and garlic cloves with some salt and a generous amount of black pepper and fry for a few minutes over a moderate heat. Stir in the tomato purée and chopped parsley and cook for a minute longer, then return the meat to the pan with any resulting juices.

Make a bouquet of the bay, thyme and orange peel and bury it in the pot with the cinnamon sticks. Heat the red wine, then pour it over the meat and add enough water or stock to bring the level of the liquid to no more than an inch below the surface of the meat. Cover the meat with an inner lid made of foil and then a close-fitting pan lid. Turn the heat to very low or place in a slow oven (150°C/gas mark 2). It will take around 3 hours to cook, but I would cook it for 2 hours one day, refrigerate it and then finish it the next. Garnish with lots of roughly chopped parsley.

BRAISED GARLIC CHICKEN
POLLO AL AJILLO **CARLOS VARGAS**

I love this way of cooking chicken because it's simple and tasty. Cook this dish slowly and you will notice an amazing distinction of flavours. First the aromatic bay, then the garlic, whose power is lessened by the alcohol, and finally the sherry, typical of southern Spain. *Pollo al ajillo* goes well with roast potatoes or with Coriander Rice (see page 188).

100ml/3½fl oz olive oil
1 large corn-fed chicken, jointed
2 heads garlic, separated into cloves but not
  peeled
3 bay leaves
500ml/18fl oz dry sherry
250ml/8fl oz water
salt and freshly ground black pepper

Heat the olive oil in a large, deep pan and brown the chicken pieces all over on a medium heat. Take out the chicken, then add the garlic and bay to the pan and fry gently until golden. Add the sherry, return the chicken to the pan and add the water. Bring to a simmer, then reduce the heat and cook slowly for 35 minutes or until the chicken is done, stirring it every few minutes to spread the garlic flavour. Season to taste.

If you're going to eat this with roast potatoes, put the chicken on top of the potatoes and then thicken the sauce by turning up the heat and boiling off some of the liquid. Pour it over the chicken and serve.

POT ROAST QUAIL WITH POMEGRANATES CORDONICES CON GRANADAS

GEORGE MANNERS

SERVES 4

Although quails and pomegranates are used together in Persian cooking, this is a Spanish dish, whose origins lie in Catalunya. The sweet meat of the quails is offset by the bittersweet flavour of the pomegranates, and this simple combination of ingredients yields a surprisingly deep-flavoured dish.

100ml/3¹/₂fl oz olive oil
8 quails
1 white onion, finely chopped
2 garlic cloves, finely chopped
4 vine-ripened tomatoes, finely chopped
4 tablespoons white wine
2 pomegranates, seeded as best you can and slightly crushed
about 150ml/¹/₄ pint light chicken stock (hot)
a few sprigs of parsley
salt and freshly ground black pepper

In a casserole that is just big enough to hold the quails in a single layer, heat the olive oil over medium heat. Lightly season the quails, place them in the oil and cook, turning, until browned all over. Remove and keep warm. Drain off a good amount of the oil, then add the onion and garlic and cook slowly until translucent. Stir in the tomatoes and cook for 5 minutes, stirring every minute. Add the white wine, increase the heat and boil until reduced by a third. Add the juice from the pomegranates and a tablespoon of their seeds. Return the quails, upside down, to the casserole and stir them into the other ingredients. Add enough hot stock to barely cover the birds, then cover the casserole and place in an oven preheated to 160°C/gas mark 3 for about 35 minutes or until the flesh begins to soften.

This dish seems to benefit from a rest, to relax and compose itself. So remove it from the oven and let it stand for 15 minutes before serving. At this point you can strain the sauce if you like, but I prefer the chunky texture and being able to see all the ingredients. Adjust the seasoning, then place the quails on a serving dish and spoon the sauce over the top. Use the parsley and a few pomegranate seeds for garnish.

PHEASANT CASSEROLE WITH CHESTNUTS, CEPS AND BACON

DAVID EYRE

SERVES 4

A wonderful casserole for the depths of winter. The chestnuts and dried mushrooms make a dark, earthy stew that I'd serve with mashed potatoes or soft polenta. Dried chestnuts, which must be soaked for an hour before they reach the pot, are a good thing to have in your storecupboard. Fresh ones will need to be roasted and peeled – a laborious and often painful way to spend time in the kitchen. Vacuum-packed chestnuts are the stuff of chefs' dreams; they are already cooked and peeled and are definitely a good thing. If you use either roasted or vacuum-packed chestnuts, they should be added to the pot towards the last half hour of cooking.

75g/3oz dried ceps (sold as porcini *in Italian grocers)*
2 large pheasant, cut into 4 pieces each
1 tablespoon olive oil
1 tablespoon butter
200g/7oz smoked fat bacon, chopped
2 celery sticks, chopped
4 garlic cloves, chopped
1 onion, chopped
1 carrot, chopped
a glass of red wine
a bouquet of sage, bay, parsley and thyme
20 vacuum-packed, dried or fresh chestnuts, prepared as described above
a good bunch of parsley, chopped
salt and freshly ground black pepper

Soak the dried ceps in some warm water. Meanwhile, season the pheasant pieces and brown them well in the olive oil in a heavy casserole. Remove the pheasant, turn the heat down and melt the butter in the pan. Add the bacon, celery, garlic, onion and carrot, then cover and cook gently for about 10 minutes, until softened. Now add the red wine, bouquet of herbs, drained soaked mushrooms, and the chestnuts, if using soaked dried ones. Return the fowl to the casserole, trying to arrange the pieces in a single layer, and add enough of the mushroom-soaking water to almost cover the pheasant. Cover the pan again and cook slowly for around $1\frac{1}{2}$ hours, adding vacuum-packed or cooked fresh chestnuts after about an hour. It doesn't matter if the chestnuts collapse but they will thicken the sauce if they do. Adjust the seasoning and stir in the chopped parsley before serving.

BRAISED GOAT WITH ROSEMARY, TOMATOES AND WINE COZIDO DE CABRITO

TRISH HILFERTY

SERVES 6–8

Kid or young goat is a much underappreciated meat in the UK. The texture of its pale flesh is not unlike milk-fed veal or spring lamb, while the flavour is slightly stronger. The prime cuts, such as saddle and leg, are good for roasting or grilling. Treat them as you would lamb. The neck and shoulder, or even a whole small animal, are delicious slowly roasted with wine and aromatics. This casserole makes good use of the cheaper cuts.

100ml/ 3¹/₂fl oz olive oil
3kg/6¹/₂lb goat shoulder or neck, on the bone
2 large onions, chopped
4 carrots, chopped
4 celery sticks, chopped
8–10 garlic cloves, sliced
500g/1lb 2oz tomatoes, chopped
250g/9oz black olives, pitted
2 bay leaves
a sprig of thyme
4–5 stalks of rosemary
450ml/³/₄ pint white wine
salt and freshly ground black pepper

Heat the oil in a large, heavy-based casserole, add the goat and brown all over. Remove the meat from the pan. Add the onions, carrots and celery and fry until lightly golden. Add the garlic, tomatoes, olives and herbs, then return the meat to the pan and pour the wine over it to come two-thirds of the way up the meat – if necessary, top up with water. Bring to a simmer, add a good pinch of salt and a grinding of black pepper, then cover and transfer to an oven preheated to 160°C/gas mark 3. Cook for around 2 hours, then remove the lid and cook for another 30 minutes or so, until the meat is falling away from the bone. The liquid should be slightly reduced, the meat crusty and brown on top and melting underneath.

Serve with potatoes – boiled, steamed or mashed.

HARE CASSEROLE
TRISH HILFERTY

SERVES 8–10

This makes a good, rich winter evening meal. Don't omit the chocolate, which is essential to thicken and enrich the casserole. The beauty of this dish is that it really looks after itself. It is best reheated the next day, as it develops a fuller flavour overnight. Any leftovers can be stripped from the bone and served with pappardelle to make one of the finest pasta dishes ever.

To joint the hares, follow the bone structure: remove the front and back legs and chop the saddle into 3 or 4 pieces, keeping the liver and kidneys intact. Try to keep as much of the blood as you can. Alternatively, you can ask your butcher to joint the hares and save the blood for you.

2 good-sized hares (around 1.5kg/3¼lb each) jointed (see above)
2 white onions, cut into chunks
3 carrots, cut into chunks
2 celery sticks, cut into chunks
2 leeks, cut into chunks
8–10 garlic cloves, chopped
2 bay leaves
a sprig of thyme
6 juniper berries, bruised
1 bottle of red wine
200g/7oz smoked streaky bacon in a piece, cut into big lardons
olive oil for frying
1 tablespoon plain flour
1 tablespoon tomato purée
50g/2oz dark chocolate (about 70% cocoa solids), finely chopped
salt and freshly ground black pepper

Put the hare, chopped vegetables, garlic, herbs and juniper in a large dish, pour over the red wine to cover (top up with water if necessary), then leave to marinate overnight.

The next day, strain the meat through a colander, keeping the wine. Pat the meat dry. Sauté the bacon gently in a heavy casserole until it releases its fat. Add the vegetables and garlic from the marinade and sauté until golden, then remove from the pan.

Add some olive oil to the pan and brown the hare in it in batches. Remove from the pan and set aside. Deglaze the pan with some of the reserved marinade, then, over a low heat, add the flour, tomato purée and blood and stir until combined and thickened. Tuck in the hare and vegetables, add the herbs from the marinade and pour in the remaining wine. The hare and vegetables should be barely covered with the wine; if necessary, top up with a little water. Add the chopped chocolate, a good pinch of salt and a grinding of black pepper. Cover tightly, then transfer to an oven preheated to 160°C/gas mark 3 and cook for about 2½ hours, until the meat is coming away from the bones. The exact cooking time will depend on the age of the hare – older animals take longer. Eat with mash.

SIDE DISHES

A BIT ON THE SIDE

Because the cooking at the Eagle is based on one plate eating, you will never find a list of side orders on our menu. However, the following recipes often appear next to our repertoire of simply grilled meats and fish. They could work as extra or alternative accompaniments to those we have suggested in previous chapters.

ROAST RED ONIONS

Red onions are best for roasting, as they cook to the most wonderful magenta colour and have a lovely sweetness, but any small firm onions or shallots, or a combination, would work.

Peel the onions and trim the hairy part of the root, but leave the main part intact to hold the onion together. Cut the onions into quarters through the root. Put them into a roasting tin with some whole peeled garlic cloves, bay leaves, strong herbs (such as thyme, rosemary, sage), a small spoonful of sugar, enough olive oil to coat everything, salt, pepper and a couple of spoonfuls of red wine vinegar. Cover the tin with foil and roast for an hour or so in a medium oven (about 180°C/gas mark 4, although the exact temperature is not that important), until the onions are tender and look done. Remove the foil and cook for a further 5 minutes. If there seems to be too much liquid, take out the onions and boil the liquid on a high flame until reduced and syrupy, then return the onions to the tin.

Roast onions are equally good cold and can be excellent with charcuterie or as part of a salad – also very good on a slice of bread when home after a busy night out.

DAVID EYRE
ROAST TOMATOES

Probably the cornerstone dish of my repertoire, these slow-roasted – almost oven-dried – tomatoes are so versatile. Not only are they superior to grilled tomatoes as something to partner grills, they are also good in pasta dishes, sauces and salads.

Halve some properly ripe tomatoes across the middle, scoop out the seeds with your fingertip and lay the tomatoes cut side up in a single layer in an ovenproof dish. Oil them slightly and season with salt, pepper, a tiny amount of sugar and some dried oregano. Depending on their intended use, you can spike them further with cumin, garlic, anchovies, chopped olives or whatever. Roast them, uncovered, at a low temperature (120–140/gas mark ¹/₂–1) for 3 hours or longer, until they look shrunken and ugly. Leave to cool. They can be kept in the fridge for a couple of weeks if you cover them in oil.

These tomatoes make a good pasta sauce when combined with whole or chopped pesto ingredients – garlic, toasted pine nuts and basil leaves. They're also good on bruschetta with anchovies or grilled sardines (see pages 115 and 58); with grilled polenta, rocket, slivered Parmesan as a starter; roughly chopped with a green chilli and some fresh coriander as a salsa for, say, grilled fish; with roasted aubergines and houmus for a lunchtime salad. With anything, really.

BRAISED PROVENÇAL VEGETABLES
RATATOUILLE KATE LEWIS

This classic Provençal dish is often made badly. The main point to note is that the vegetables should be cut into largish pieces and fried separately. It makes a great lunch with crusty bread or goat's cheese. Alternatively serve it as an accompaniement to grilled or roast meat or fish.

The Catalan equivalent of ratatouille is *samfaina*, which is identical except that the vegetables are cut into thin slices. *Samfaina* is only ever served as an accompaniment.

4–5 tablespoons olive oil
2 courgettes, roughly chopped
2 onions, roughly chopped
2 garlic cloves, sliced
2 red or green peppers, roughly chopped
2 aubergines, roughly chopped
400g/14oz tin of tomatoes (preferably organic)
a small bunch of oregano or marjoram
2 sprigs of thyme or rosemary
1 bay leaf
a small bunch of flat-leaf parsley
salt and freshly ground black pepper

Heat 2 tablespoons of the oil in a casserole or thick-bottomed pan, add the courgettes and season with salt and pepper. Fry until lightly coloured, then remove from the pan and set aside. Heat another tablespoon of the oil in the pan, add the onions and garlic, then season and cook gently for 5–10 minutes until soft. Add the remaining oil to the pan, then stir in the peppers and aubergines, season, and cook over a medium heat until lightly coloured. Add the courgettes, tomatoes, the leaves from the oregano or marjoram, the rosemary or thyme and the bay. Stew gently for 30 minutes. Taste for seasoning and then stir in the whole parsley leaves. Serve hot or at room temperature.

BROCCOLI AND TREVISO WITH ANCHOVY DRESSING TRISH HILFERTY

SERVES 4–6

This recipe creates a big batch of dressing. It keeps for ages in the fridge and makes a great Caesar-type salad with Cos lettuce and Parmesan, a dip for raw vegetables, or a spread for hot toast. It can also be served with fish such as sea bass, bream or hake.

3 heads broccoli
2 heads of radicchio di Treviso

For the dressing
150g/5oz cured anchovies in olive oil
2 garlic cloves, chopped
2 teaspoons Dijon mustard
1 tablespoon sherry vinegar
350ml/12fl oz olive oil
1 teaspoon freshly ground black pepper
1 small red chilli, chopped
a handful of basil, chopped

Purée the anchovies, garlic, mustard and vinegar in a food processor until smooth. With the machine running, add the oil very slowly, as if making mayonnaise. Season with the black pepper, then pulse in the chilli and basil.

Divide the broccoli into florets, then peel the stems and slice them into chunks. Separate the Treviso into leaves. Bring a large pot of salted water to the boil. Blanch the broccoli florets in it briefly (perhaps 1 minute) because they have to be crunchy, then remove with a slotted spoon and shake off excess water. Repeat with the stalks, cooking them for longer if necessary. Toss the broccoli with the Treviso and enough of the dressing to coat it lightly.

SICILIAN AUBERGINE RELISH
CAPONATA KATE LEWIS

SERVES 4

Caponata was originally made in summer and bottled for winter use. It is delicious on bruschetta (see page 54) or as a sweet and sour relish with cold meats or cheese. Use good quality tinned tomatoes unless you find fabulous fresh ones.

2 onions, chopped
150ml/¹⁄₄ pint extra virgin olive oil
2 celery sticks, cut into 1–2cm/¹⁄₂–³⁄₄-inch
*   pieces*
400g/14oz tin of plum tomatoes (squash
*   them thoroughly in a colander and discard*
*   the juice)*
75g/3oz green olives
2 tablespoons salted capers, soaked in cold
*   water for 30 minutes and then squeezed*
20g/³⁄₄oz caster sugar
3 tablespoons white wine vinegar
2 aubergines, cut into 1–2 cm/¹⁄₂–³⁄₄-inch
*   cubes*
salt and freshly ground black pepper

Season the onions and fry them gently in 3 tablespoons of the olive oil until soft. Add the celery and cook for 3 minutes. Increase the heat, add the tomatoes and simmer until reduced to a thick consistency. Add the olives, capers, sugar and vinegar and simmer gently for 20 minutes, stirring from time to time.

Heat the remaining olive oil in a large frying pan. Season the aubergine and sauté in the oil over a medium heat until lightly browned and cooked through. Lift out with a slotted spoon and add to the other vegetables. Taste and adjust the seasoning.

Serve at room temperature. Caponata will keep for weeks in the fridge if covered with oil.

FRIED CHORICITOS WITH PIMENTOS, AGUADIENTE AND GARLIC
CHORIZO A LA LLAMA DAVID EYRE

SERVES 4

The Spanish name for this dish is a bit of a mystery – no-one seems to know of its origins. Choricitos are diminutive chorizos sold linked together.

Cut 8 soft choricitos on the bias into slices 2cm/³/₄-inch thick. Heat a heavy frying pan and gently fry them in a little olive oil until cooked through and well coloured. Turn the heat up, add a splash of aguadiente or brandy and ignite it (standing well back), then let the alcohol burn off. As the flames die, add 2 sliced cloves of garlic and 4 or more roasted pimientos (preferably wood-roasted red piquillo peppers, which are sold oil-packed in tins, or you could roast and peel some small red peppers). Turn off the heat when the garlic slices start to colour. Add some chopped flat-leaf parsley and serve immediately, with bread. The whole operation should take no longer than ten minutes.

COOKING DRIED BEANS AND LENTILS

Dried beans and lentils are, I think, looked upon with deep suspicion by many, who imagine that they must be soaked for days, then cooked for hours to render them safe. This is simply not true. The important thing is to buy quality beans that are not years old and are from a reputable source. The older they are, the tougher they will be and the longer they will take to soak and cook. The Eagle buys its beans from northern Spain, the source of the world's finest dried beans, especially butter beans and tiny white haricots. Tinned beans are okay in some dishes, but they must be washed before use.

Dried white, red and black haricots, butter and broad beans, flageolets and chickpeas all require soaking overnight (or during the working day). Drain the soaked beans and bring them to the boil in fresh water. When scum appears on the surface, drain again, then cover by 2.5cm/1 inch with cold water and bring back to a simmer. If the beans are red or black they must be boiled hard for 10 minutes; otherwise just simmer them steadily in a covered pan to achieve evenly cooked beans. Expect them to take at least 1½ hours, and add more water if the level drops below the surface of the beans. Don't add any salt until the beans are cooked, as it hardens the skin. When cooked, keep them covered in the cooking liquid with a good glug of olive oil. If you are using them in a soup, purée a cupful or two to give a creamy texture. If you are not using the beans immediately, refrigerate them as soon as they are cool.

Italian and Spanish brown lentils and the famous French, purple-tinged *lentilles du Puy* require no soaking and will take under an hour to cook. Cover them by 5cm/2 inches cold water, bring to a simmer with a couple of cloves of garlic and a stick of celery and cook until tender. Partially drain the lentils, and, whilst they are still warm, season and dress with olive oil and lemon juice. Any left over make a good basis for a salad if dressed with more lemon and olive oil, and would go very well with smoked fish.

CANNELLINI BEANS WITH GARLIC AND SAGE PEDRO CHAVES

SERVES 8

Beans often make an appearance in Mediterranean meals, accompanying grilled meats such as pork or lamb. In this recipe, the handsome cannellini bean is enhanced by the traditional flavours of sage and garlic. It is essential to use dried, but not ancient, beans and fresh herbs.

500g/1lb 2oz dried cannellini beans
a bunch of sage, leaves chopped and stalks
  kept
2 large garlic cloves, very finely chopped
1 red chilli, finely chopped
75ml/2¹/₂fl oz extra virgin olive oil
salt and freshly ground black pepper

Place the beans in a large saucepan, cover with twice as much water and leave to soak overnight.

The next day, drain the beans, cover with fresh water and bring to the boil. As soon as froth appears on the surface, remove the pan from the heat and drain. Cover the beans with fresh water again (about 2.5cm/ 1 inch above the level of the beans), add the sage stalks and bring to the boil. Cook for 1–1¹/₂ hours or until the beans are soft. Do not drain them. Place one cup of the mixture in a food processor or liquidiser, purée and return to the pot. This will give a creamy consistency to the dish. Finally, add the garlic, chilli, sage leaves, salt, pepper and olive oil. Leave to stand for 20 minutes before serving.

BRAISED PUY LENTILS
MARGOT HENDERSON

SERVES 4

Puy lentils are often thought to be the best variety of lentil as they have a distinctive peppery flavour and they hold their shape well during cooking. They have a pretty blueish-green colour and originate from the Le Puy region of France. A perfect accompaniment to plain grilled chops or sausages.

6 tablespoons extra virgin olive oil
1 onion, thinly sliced
1 fennel bulb, thinly sliced
1 leek, thinly sliced
2 garlic cloves, finely chopped
1 medium-sized loose-leaved cabbage such as Savoy or Hispi
175g/6oz Puy lentils
175ml/6fl oz white wine
1 lemon
1 tablespoon Dijon mustard
salt and freshly ground black pepper

Heat 5 tablespoons of the oil in a medium pan over a medium heat. Add the onion, fennel, leek and garlic and cook gently until soft, then add the lentils. Add the wine and reduce by half (about 5 minutes). Add enough water to the pan so that the lentils and vegetables are covered by about 2cm and cook for about 20–30 minutes. The lentils should still hold their shape when cooked but be tender.

Just before serving, stir the thinly-sliced cabbage into the lentils – it will cook in the hot lentils. Add a squeeze of lemon juice, the mustard and the remaining olive oil to the pan, stir well and season to taste just before serving.

SPINACH WITH PINE NUTS AND RAISINS JOHN HUMPHRIES

SERVES 4

This versatile dish is normally served as a starter but we use it as an accompaniment to meats and especially grilled fish. The combination of nuts and fruit in a savoury dish has a typical Catalan signature and it looks great on the plate: glossy green spinach studded with pale-gold pine nuts and plump, succulent raisins.

The anchovy, garlic and lemon work well as strong seasonings. In Spain, the spinach is boiled first. At the Eagle, we have improved on this by wilting the spinach in a wok at high speed.

1kg/2¼lb fresh spinach
2 tablespoons olive oil, preferably from Catalunya and made from Arbequina olives
25g/1oz pine nuts
1 garlic clove, very finely chopped
25g/1oz raisins, soaked in hot water for an hour or so
2 anchovy fillets, chopped
juice of 1 lemon
salt and freshly ground black pepper

Wash the spinach and remove the stalks, then shake it dry. In a wok or large pan, heat the oil over a high flame. Add the pine nuts and garlic and shake the wok. When the pine nuts start to colour, add the drained raisins and anchovies and cook for 30 seconds. Then add the spinach – at first it will fill the wok – stirring and tossing as it starts to wilt. Add some salt and pepper and the lemon juice and stir once more. Then serve on a warmed white plate, with a little more olive oil if you wish.

CELERIAC MASH OR GRATIN
TRISH HILFERTY

SERVES 6

Celeriac is such an inexpensive and underused winter vegetable. The mash is simplicity itself; you don't have to use sage but it does complement the celeriac beautifully. The gratin is also very easy, and is particularly good with lamb or can even be served alone as a starter.

CELERIAC MASH

2 heads celeriac
4 large potatoes, peeled
3 garlic cloves, peeled
300ml/¹/₂ pint milk
150g/5oz butter
a handful of sage leaves, chopped
salt and freshly ground black pepper

Peel the celeriac and cut it into chunks, dropping these into acidulated water (water with a squeeze of lemon) as you go. Cut the potatoes into chunks about twice the size of the celeriac – they cook much faster. Boil the potatoes and the celeriac, along with the garlic cloves, in plenty of salted water until tender. Drain really well, return to the pot and dry off any excess moisture over a very low heat. Heat the milk, then pour it into the pot and crush the vegetables with a potato masher. Beat in the butter, fold in the sage and season with pepper. Check for salt.

CELERIAC GRATIN

250ml/8fl oz double cream
10 sage leaves
2 bay leaves
3 garlic cloves, thinly sliced
3 tablespoons freshly grated Parmesan cheese
3 medium-sized celeriac, peeled and cut into
*   slices 5mm/¹/₄-inch thick*
sea salt and freshly ground black pepper

Put the cream in a pan with the herbs, garlic and Parmesan and simmer until it has reduced a little. Arrange the sliced celeriac in an ovenproof dish as densely as possible to a depth of 3–4cm/1¹/₄–1¹/₂ inches, seasoning each layer. Pour over the cream. Cover with foil and cook in a medium-hot oven (200°C/gas mark 6) for around 30 minutes or until the celeriac just yields to the tip of a knife. Brown the top under a hot grill if you wish.

CELERIAC REMOULADE

HARRY LESTER

SERVES 6

This is a classic French favourite of fine strips of celeriac dressed with a mustard mayonnaise. Serve it as starter with crusty bread or as an accompaniment to charcuterie or cold roast beef.

1 small celeriac
3 free-range medium egg yolks
2–3 tablespoons Dijon mustard
1 tablespoon white wine vinegar
750ml/1¼ pints sunflower oil
salt

Using a mandolin or a food processor with the appropriate attachment, cut the celeriac into long fine strips. Place the strips in a colander and lightly season them with a pinch of salt. Set aside while you make the mayonnaise.

Place the egg yolks, mustard and vinegar in a food processor bowl or a mixing bowl and blend or whisk until well combined. Gradually drizzle the oil through the feeder tube of the food processor with the motor running or into the mixing bowl, whisking continually, until it has all been used up. Mix the celeriac strips into the mayonnaise.

VARIATIONS

As an alternative to mustard-flavoured mayonnaise add one of the following to the mayo once you have added all the oil: 1 tablespoon of drained and rinsed, finely chopped capers; 1 tablespoon of finely chopped gherkins; or 1 tablespoon of finely chopped soft herbs, such as flat-leaf parsley, chervil, tarragon or chives.

JANSSON'S TEMPTATION
TRISH HILFERTY

This traditional Swedish dish goes very well with roast lamb.

8 large waxy potatoes, peeled
50g/2oz butter
2 onions, sliced
2 garlic cloves, thinly sliced
300ml/¹/₂ pint milk
300ml/¹/₂ pint double cream
75g/3oz anchovies in oil, drained
salt and freshly ground black pepper

Slice the potatoes fairly thinly, to about 5mm/¹/₄ inch. Grease a baking dish with 20g/³/₄oz of the butter. Melt the remaining butter in a large pan and sweat the onions in it until soft. Stir in the garlic and potatoes, then pour in the milk and cream. Tip in the anchovies and mix well, making sure they are evenly distributed. Adjust the seasoning.

Tip the whole lot into the baking dish and bake in an oven preheated to 200°C/gas mark 6 for 1 hour or until the potatoes are tender. If the top is browning too quickly, cover the dish with foil.

OVEN POTATOES
PATATAS AL FORNO DAVID EYRE

Not really a gratin, since it doesn't include cheese, but potatoes baked in a shallow dish in this way were used to partner grilles and roasts almost every day when I was at the Eagle. Endless fun can be had with the flavours added to the potatoes (see suggestions below). Use any waxy potato varieties; floury baking potatoes will collapse into a mush. The Cyprus *Nicola* potato is the ideal but Maris Piper is a good second choice.

sufficient potatoes, peeled and sliced
*   5mm/^{1}/$_4$-inch thick, to fill and ovenproof*
*   dish to a depth of 4cm/1^1/$_4$ inches*
1 large onion for every 500g/1lb 2oz
*   potatoes, sliced*
olive oil
salt and freshly ground black pepper

Additional ingredients as you think fit
pitted black olives and garlic
parsley and garlic
sliced green or red peppers and garlic
chopped rosemary and/or sage
smoked streaky bacon
saffron

In a large bowl, mix the potatoes and onions with enough olive oil to coat them lightly. Layer them in the ovenproof dish, with whichever additions you are using. Cover with foil and bake in a moderate oven (about 180/gas mark4, although the exact temperature is not important) for up to an hour, until nearly cooked. Remove the foil and brown the top for 15 minutes.

POTATOES WITH BRAISED CABBAGE

TOM NORRINGTON-DAVIES

SERVES 6

This is a great accompaniment to winter roasts but it could also be eaten on its own, since the pancetta provides a good meat fix. Duck fat, bacon and cabbage is a famously good trinity, so why wait for bubble and squeak tomorrow when you can have this today?

3 tablespoons duck fat
8 large waxy potatoes, peeled and cut into thick rounds
300g/11oz smoked pancetta, roughly diced
a handful of sage leaves, very roughly chopped
1 teaspoon juniper berries, crushed
3 onions, chopped
2 garlic cloves, chopped
1 Savoy cabbage, darker green leaves only (cavolo nero in season would be even better), roughly chopped
salt and freshly ground black pepper

Heat 2 tablespoons of the duck fat in a roasting tray and let it get really hot. Add the potato slices and stir until they all have a good coating of fat. Place in an oven preheated to 200°C/gas mark 6.

Heat the remaining fat in a wide pan or casserole. Add the pancetta, sage, juniper berries, onions and garlic and fry on a high heat for a couple of minutes. Stir in the cabbage and add about 250ml/8fl oz of water. Season with salt and pepper, then cover and cook gently, stirring occasionally. The potatoes will take about half an hour, by which time the cabbage mixture should be good and ready. You now add one dish to the other. For sheer visual effect, adding the cabbage to the potatoes is my favourite. Mix it all thoroughly. Do not worry if some of the potatoes break up a little. You can shove it back in the oven to crisp the top layer up ever so slightly, but the dish will keep warm enough to serve for ages.

3 POTATO SALADS

DAVID EYRE

SERVES 4

You need to choose your potatoes carefully for salads. The first two salads here use waxy new potatoes such as the ubiquitous Charlottes, my beloved *Rattes*, also known as *Belle de Fontenay*, Pink Fir Apples, Jersey Royals or small *Nicola* potatoes from Cyprus. The third can be made with any large potato apart from those suitable for baking (King Edward and the like), which will collapse when boiling. By all means peel them after boiling, when still warm, but I can never really see that the effort is justified.

WITH MAYONNAISE, CAPERS AND ONION

500g/1lb 2oz new potatoes, scrubbed
2 egg yolks
1 teaspoon mustard
400ml/14fl oz sunflower oil
1 teaspoon white wine vinegar
1 tablespoon salted capers, washed and soaked in several changes of cold water for 1 hour
1 red onion, very finely chopped
1 tablespoon chopped parsley
salt and freshly ground black pepper

Put the potatoes on to boil in salted water. Meanwhile, make the mayonnaise. Beat the egg yolks and mustard together in a food processor or mixer, then add the oil in the slowest possible stream with the machine running. Add the vinegar at the end and season to taste. Then thin with a tablespoon of water.

Drain the potatoes and cut them into pieces. Combine with all the other ingredients and the mayonnaise while still warm.

WITH GREEN OLIVES, SHALLOTS AND SWEET HERBS

500g/1lb 2oz new potatoes, scrubbed
3 shallots, very finely chopped
100g/4oz green olives, roughly chopped
1 garlic clove, crushed and finely chopped
2 tablespoons chopped mixed herbs such as mint, chervil, tarragon, parsley, marjoram, basil
4 tablespoons olive oil
1 tablespoon balsamic vinegar
salt and freshly ground black pepper

Boil the potatoes until tender, then drain. Mix together the rest of the ingredients. Cut the potatoes into pieces and combine with the other ingredients while still warm. Season to taste.

WITH BLACK OLIVES, SPRING ONIONS AND OLIVE OIL

500g/1lb 2oz potatoes (see left), scrubbed (peeled if you wish)
100g/4oz black olives, roughly chopped
6 tablespoons olive oil
a small bunch of spring onions, chopped
freshly ground black pepper

Boil the potatoes until tender, then drain. Cut them into slices and bruise in a colander. Gently mix together with the other ingredients.

CORIANDER RICE

TOM NORRINGTON-DAVIES

SERVES 6

Some things go with nothing better than a fluffy serving of white rice. In particular, some of our wetter dishes are grateful for it – such as Octopus Stew (see page 121), lamb shanks or Pollo al Ajillo (see page 158) – as are fish (mackerel is the best) with a really simple salsa or salad leaves.

Here we deviate from the sticky rice of Spain and Italy. Basmati is best. The name means 'fragrant', and it should have a slightly nutty, perfumed smell. Only rice grown in the Himilayan foothills of India and Pakistan should be labelled basmati. The soil and water in this region give it its special aroma and flavour. So choose a reputable brand, such as Tilda, because there is a huge difference between this and other kinds of long-grain rice. This dish is our own very deconstructed and not remotely authentic pilaff. If you have problems cooking rice, use this basic absorption method for plain basmati as well – it never fails.

4 tablespoons olive oil
1 clove
$^1/_2$ teaspoon cumin seeds
enough basmati rice to fill a measuring jug
  to the 750ml/1$^1/_4$ pint level
1.5 litres/2$^1/_2$ pints water
juice of $^1/_2$ lemon
a bunch of coriander, very roughly chopped
salt and freshly ground black pepper

Nowadays you do not need to wash basmati rice. For this dish, however, we give it a very brief toasting. Heat 2 tablespoons of the oil in a pan (choose one with a very tight-fitting lid). Add the clove and cumin seeds, then add the rice and stir thoroughly until it is coated with the oil and looks a little opaque. Add all the water and turn the heat up full. Bring the water just to boiling point, then turn the heat down as low as it will go. The water should be just below a simmer. Cover with the lid; it must fit snugly. The rice will carry on cooking in the steam once it has absorbed all the water. Don't stir! After 10 minutes, taste a grain and see if it is as soft as you want it. As soon as it is, remove the pan from the heat, add the remaining oil and gently nudge the rice apart with a carving fork, a narrow knife or a skewer. Don't use a spoon, which would be like a bull in a china shop and smash the grains (unlike other rice, basmati elongates rather than thickens, so it is delicate). Fold in the lemon juice and coriander, add salt and pepper to taste and serve.

INDEX